Focus in Grades 3–5

Teaching with Curriculum Focal Points

Focus in Grades 3–5

Teaching with Curriculum Focal Points

3–5

Amy Mirra

NCTM | NATIONAL COUNCIL OF
TEACHERS OF MATHEMATICS

Copyright © 2008 by
THE NATIONAL COUNCIL OF TEACHERS OF MATHEMATICS, INC.
1906 Association Drive, Reston, VA 20191-1502
(703) 620-9840; (800) 235-7566; www.nctm.org

Library of Congress Cataloging-in-Publication Data

Mirra, Amy.
    Teaching with curriculum focal points : focus in grades 3–5 / by Amy Mirra.
        p. cm.
    Includes bibliographical references.
    ISBN 978-0-87353-609-7
    1. Mathematics—Study and teaching (Elementary)—United
States—Standards. 2. Education—Curricula—United States—Standards.
3. Curriculum planning—United States—Standards. 4. School management
and organization—United States. I. Title.
    QA135.6.M565 2008
    372.7—dc22
                                              200801225

The National Council of Teachers of Mathematics is a public voice of mathematics education, providing vision, leadership, and professional development to support teachers in ensuring mathematics learning of the highest quality for all students.

Printed in the United States of America

Contents

Contents — Continued

On September 12, 2006, the National Council of Teachers of Mathematics released *Curriculum Focal Points for Prekindergarten through Grade 8 Mathematics: A Quest for Coherence* to encourage discussions at the national, state, and district levels on the importance of designing a coherent elementary school mathematics curriculum focusing on the important mathematical ideas at each grade level. The natural question that followed the release of *Curriculum Focal Points* was "How do we translate this view of a focused curriculum into classroom practice?"

Focus in Grades 3–5, one in a series of three grade-band publications, is designed to support teachers, supervisors, and coordinators as they begin the discussion of a more focused curriculum across and within kindergarten through eighth grade, as presented in *Curriculum Focal Points.* Additionally, teacher educators should find it useful as a vehicle for exploring issues involving the grades 3–5 mathematics curriculum with their preservice teachers.

The members of the development team, all active professional development leaders, designed a detailed outline for *Focus in Grades 3–5.* We highlighted the need for new depth and coherence within the content at each of grades 3, 4, and 5; the importance of connections across the content areas in grades 3–5; and implications for learning, practice, and assessment suggested by a focused curriculum. The author of *Focus in Grades 3–5,* guided by our outline, created this grade-band book as a framework for lesson-study-type experiences that involve identifying focus in an existing curriculum or creating focus in a curriculum that is soon to be under revision.

Our intention for this publication is that it will be a model for professional development that supports the implementation of a more coherent and focused mathematics curriculum by posing questions that facilitate discussion and decision making. Whether you engage in reflective discussions with your colleagues or simply use these questions to stimulate independent reflection on your own instructional planning, we hope that your thinking leads you to a view of elementary mathematics teaching that fosters in all students the depth of understanding of important mathematical concepts necessary for their future success.

—Jane M. Schielack, for the
CFP Grade-Band 3–5 Development Team

As states and local school districts implement more rigorous assessment and accountability systems, teachers often face long lists of mathematics topics or learning expectations to address at each grade level, with many topics repeating from year to year. Lacking clear, consistent priorities and focus, teachers stretch to find the time to present important mathematical topics effectively and in depth.

The National Council of Teachers of Mathematics (NCTM) is responding to this challenge by presenting *Curriculum Focal Points for Prekindergarten through Grade 8 Mathematics: A Quest for Coherence*. Building on *Principles and Standards for School Mathematics* (NCTM 2000), this new publication is offered as a starting point in a dialogue on what is important at particular levels of instruction and as an initial step toward a more coherent, focused curriculum in this country.

The writing team for *Curriculum Focal Points for Prekindergarten through Grade 8 Mathematics* consisted of nine members, with at least one university-level mathematics educator or mathematician and one pre-K–8 classroom practitioner from each of the three grade bands (pre-K–grade 2, grades 3–5, and grades 6–8). The writing team examined curricula from multiple states and countries as well as a wide array of researchers' and experts' writings in creating a set of focal points for pre-K–grade 8 mathematics.

On behalf of the Board of Directors, we thank everyone who helped make this publication possible.

Cathy Seeley
President, 2004–2006
National Council of Teachers of Mathematics

Francis (Skip) Fennell
President, 2006–2008
National Council of Teachers of Mathematics

Members of the Curriculum Focal Points for Grades PK–8 Writing Team

Jane F. Schielack, *Chair,* Texas A&M University, College Station, Texas
Sybilla Beckman, University of Georgia, Athens, Georgia
Randall I. Charles, San José State University (emeritus), San José, California
Douglas H. Clements, University at Buffalo, State University of New York, Buffalo, New York
Paula B. Duckett, District of Columbia Public Schools (retired), Washington, D.C.
Francis (Skip) Fennell, McDaniel College, Westminster, Maryland
Sharon L. Lewandowski, Bryant Woods Elementary School, Columbia, Maryland
Emma Treviño, Charles A. Dana Center, University of Texas at Austin, Austin, Texas
Rose Mary Zbiek, The Pennsylvania State University, University Park, Pennsylvania

Staff Liaison
Melanie S. Ott, National Council of Teachers of Mathematics, Reston, Virginia

ACKNOWLEDGMENTS

The National Council of Teachers of Mathematics and the author would like to thank the following individuals of the CFP Grade-Band 3–5 Development Team for developing a detailed outline for the content of this publication and for their reviews of, and feedback on, drafts of the manuscript. The author especially thanks Janie Schielack for all her time and support, her invaluable guidance and advice, and her continuing commitment to the Curriculum Focal Points project. We also wish to thank the Grade–5 Development Team for their contributions to the ideas of the outline. We extend a special thank-you to Bonnie Ennis for also gathering the student work samples.

CFP Grade-Band 3–5 Development Team

Jane F. Schielack, *Chair*
Texas A&M University

Bonnie Ennis
Wicomico County (Maryland) Board of Education

Susan Friel
University of North Carolina

Steve Klass
San Diego State University

CFP Grade 5 Development Team

Sybilla Beckmann, *Chair*
University of Georgia

Karen C. Fuson
Northwestern University

John SanGiovanni
Howard County (Maryland) Public Schools

Thomasenia L. Adams
University of Florida

We would also like to thank Richard Askey, University of Wisconsin—Madison; Francis (Skip) Fennel, NCTM President; and James Rubillo, NCTM Executive Director, for their thoughtful reviews of, and helpful comments on, the manuscript. The final product reflects the editorial and design expertise of Ann Butterfield, NCTM senior editor, and Randy White, NCTM production manager.

Introduction

Purpose of This Guide

Your first question when looking at NCTM's Curriculum Focal Points might be, *How can I use NCTM's Focal Points with the local and state curriculum I am expected to teach?* The intent of this guide is to help instructional leaders and classroom teachers build focus into the curriculum that they are expected to teach through connecting related ideas and prioritizing topics of emphasis at each grade level. NCTM's Curriculum Focal Points document is not intended to be a national curriculum but has been developed to help bring more consistency to mathematics curricula across the country. Collectively, it constitutes a framework of how curriculum might be organized at each grade level, prekindergarten through grade 8. It is also intended to help bring about discussion within and across states and school districts about the important mathematical ideas to be taught at each grade level. Because of the current variation among states' curricula, the Curriculum Focal Points are not likely to match up perfectly with any state curriculum. This volume, a guide to the Focal Points for grades 3–5, explores instruction that supports a focused curriculum, as well as looks at the impact of focal points on assessment. Additional grade-level books for each grade band will be developed by NCTM to help teachers translate the focal points identified for their grade level into coherent and meaningful instruction. Taken together, this 3–5 grade-band guide and the individual grade-level books for grades 3, 4, and 5 can be used for teachers' professional development experiences as well as by individual classroom teachers.

Purpose of Curriculum Focal Points

The mathematics curriculum in the United States has often been characterized as a "mile wide and an inch deep." Many topics are studied each year—often reviewing much that was covered in previous years—and little depth is added each time the topic is addressed. In contrast, higher performing countries tend to select a few fundamental topics each year and develop them in more depth. In addition, because education has always been locally controlled in the United States, learning expectations can significantly differ by state and local school systems.

In the 1980s, the National Council of Teachers of Mathematics began the process of bringing about change to school mathematics programs, particularly with the first document to outline standards in mathematics titled *Curriculum and Evaluation Standards* (NCTM 1989). This document provided major direction to states and school districts in developing their curricula. NCTM's *Principles and Standards for School Mathematics* (NCTM 2000) further elaborated on the ideas of the 1989 Standards outlining learning expectations in the grade bands of pre-K–2, 3–5, 6–8, and 9–12. *Principles*

> *A curriculum is more than a collection of activities: It must be coherent, focused on important mathematics, and well articulated across the grades."*
>
> —The Curriculum Principle,
> *Principles and Standards for School Mathematics*

> The intent of this guide is to help instructional leaders and classroom teachers build focus into the curriculum that they are expected to teach through connecting related ideas and prioritizing topics of emphasis at each grade level.

and Standards also highlighted six principles, which included the Curriculum Principle, to provide guidance for developing mathematical programs. The Curriculum Principle emphasized the need to link with, and build on, mathematical ideas as students progress through the grades, deepening their mathematical knowledge over time.

NCTM's *Curriculum Focal Points for Prekindergarten through Grade 8 Mathematics: A Quest for Coherence* (NCTM 2006) is the next step in helping states and local districts refocus their curriculum. It provides an example of a focused and coherent curriculum in prekindergarten through grade 8 by identifying the most important mathematical topics or "focal points" at each grade level. The focal points are not discrete topics to be taught and checked off, but rather a cluster of related knowledge, skills, and concepts. By organizing and prioritizing curriculum and instruction in grades pre-K–8 around focus points at each grade level, teachers can foster more-cumlulative learning of mathematics by students, and students' work in the later grades will build on and deepen what they learned in the earlier grades. Organizing mathematics content in this way will help ensure a solid mathematical foundation for high school mathematics and beyond.

> The Focal Points provide an example of a focused and coherent curriculum in prekindergarten through grade 8 by identifying the most important mathematical topics or "focal points" at each grade level.

Impact of Focal Points on Curriculum, Instruction, and Assessment

Significant improvement can be made in the areas of curriculum, instruction, and assessment by identifying focal points at each grade level. At the curriculum level, focal points will allow for more rigorous and in-depth study of important mathematics in each grade. This rigor will translate to a more meaningful curriculum that students can understand and apply, thereby ensuring student learning and an increase in student achievement. At the instructional level, focal points will allow teachers to more fully know the core topics they are responsible for teaching. Teachers will not necessarily be teaching *less* or *more* but will be able to teach *better*. Professional Development could also be tailored to deepen teachers' knowledge of these focal points and connect these ideas in meaningful ways. Assessments could be designed that truly measure students' mastery of core topics rather than survey a broad range of disparate topics, thus allowing for closer monitoring of student development. At the classroom assessment level, having a smaller number of essential topics will help teachers determine what their students have learned and provide sufficient time to ensure that these topics have been learned deeply enough to use and build on in the following years. If state assessments are more focused as well, more detailed information can be gathered for districts and schools on areas for improvement.

Questions to Reflect On

- **What does it mean to progress rather than "spiral" in learning?**
- **What are some of the major learning progressions that occur in grades 3–5?**
- **How are basic facts and algorithms addressed in a focused curriculum?**

You may feel overwhelmed with the wide range of mathematical topics you are expected to teach over a given year. Pressure to cover all of these topics and also prepare students for mandated state assessments is usually a major concern for many teachers. NCTM's Curriculum Focal Points is not intended to add to the already long list of concepts and skills presented in your state and local curriculum. Instead, its Focal Points for grades 3–5 can be used along with this guide to focus your own curriculum into major areas of emphasis at each grade level.

Concept of a Focal Point and Connections

A mathematics curriculum organized around focal points highlights the most important mathematical ideas for each grade and presents these essential ideas as interconnected packages of related knowledge, skills, and concepts. Students gain extended experiences with these core concepts and skills with the ultimate goal of promoting deeper mathematical understanding and connections among mathematical ideas. The majority of instruction is organized around the identified focal points for that grade, however, this emphasis does not mean that those focus areas are the only topics presented during that year. NCTM's focal points also include "Connections to the Focal Points," which are just that—related ideas and concepts that connect with the focal points identified. The Connections serve a number of purposes. First, the connections might highlight introductory experiences for that particular grade level to build a foundation for a future focal point. For example, although fluency with division of whole numbers is not a focal point in grade 4, students begin to develop initial understandings of, and strategies for, multidigit division in this grade. Connections can also serve to highlight continuing experiences of a focal point identified at a previous level. For example, students in grade 3 continue to make connections to the place-value concepts they focused on in grade 2 by extending their repertoire to numbers up to 10,000. The Connections also help build relationships among content strands. For example, although the Measurement content strand is not a focal point in grade 3, measurement can be a context for the study of fractions in grade 3 as students measure with fractional parts of linear units, and for their study of two-dimensional shapes as students measure the perimeter. See Appendixes A, B, and C for the complete listing and descriptions of the curriculum focal points and connections identified by NCTM for grades 3, 4, and 5. The curriculum focal points for other grades as well as the complete document *Curriculum Focal Points for Prekindergarten through Grade 8 Mathematics* can be viewed on NCTM's Web site at www.nctm.org or ordered for purchase.

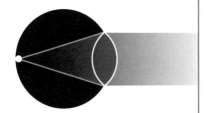

BUILDING FOCUS TASK: *Think about your own grade level or one particular grade level. What are some of the fundamental mathematical ideas or topics that build a foundation for later learning? How do those mathematical ideas or topics connect to learning in later grades?*

Learning Progressions and Examples

The goal of a curriculum organized around focal points is that students' mathematical knowledge progresses and deepens over time. A focused curriculum emphasises depth of understanding as well as connections among mathematical ideas. Students do not simply repeat previously learned topics or forget about topics they learned in previous grades. Instead, the identified focal points for a particular grade level build on the focal points from the previous grade, and at the same time lead the way for the focal points for the following grade.

> The identified focal points for a particular grade level build on the focal points from the previous grade, and at the same time lead the way for the focal points for the following grade.

Example of the Learning Progression for Division

As an example of a learning progression, let us take a look at how students' understanding of division progresses or develops over time. Although division is not identified as a focal point in the pre-K–2 years, children begin to develop some initial understanding of division concepts during this time. In particular, students in these early grades develop understanding of division as it relates to sharing or creating equal groups. They may act out division situations. For example, students might act out the following scenarios using concrete materials:

- Four children want to share 8 balloons
- Three children want to share 12 balloons
- Two children want to share 12 balloons
- Six children want to share 12 balloons
- Two children want to share 10 balloons

(Source: *Navigating through Number and Operations in Grades Pre-K–2* (NCTM 2004, p. 54). Reprinted with permission.

In the sharing model for division also known as the "partition" model, the number of groups is known, but the size of each group is not known. During these foundational experiences, children might try to make equal groups through trial and error or by dealing out a balloon to each child one at a time until no more balloons remain.

In grade 3, division becomes a focal point as it relates to "Developing understanding of multiplication and division and strategies for basic multiplication facts and related division facts." Students continue to use the sharing or partitioning model to understand division as well as the repeated subtraction model for division. In the subtracting model for division, the size of the group is known but the number of groups is unknown. An example such as the bookshelf problem that follows might be encountered. To solve this problem, students might use counters to represent the 36 books and subtract out 9 counters repeatedly to determine how many groups of 9, or how many shelves, will be used.

Jeremy had 36 books to put on his shelves. He put 9 books on each shelf. How many shelves did he use for these books?

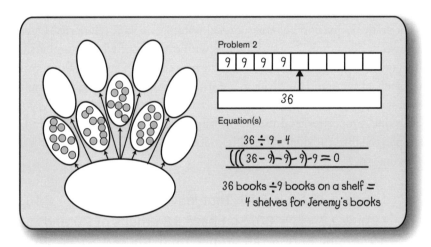

(Source: *Navigating through Number and Operations in Grades 3–5* (NCTM 2007b, p. 64). Reprinted with permission.

Students also learn that division is just another way of looking at multiplication. For example, just as 9 × 4 can be thought of as 9 groups of 4, if you have 36 pieces of candy and want to give them out to 9 children, each child will get 4 pieces of candy. Or, if you want to give 4 pieces of the candy to each child at a party, you can distribute the 36 pieces equally to 9 children.

Instruction on the basic multiplication and division facts should emphasize the use of thinking strategies rather than the simple memorization of isolated facts through rote drill. The goal is that these basic facts will become automatic, essentially become memorized, but automaticity of these facts is achieved by focusing on thinking and the relationship between the facts. For example, students will notice that 7 groups of 3 results in the same total as 3 groups of 7, thereby applying the commutative property. Students might also use known facts and their understanding of the meaning of multiplication and division to determine unknown facts, such as that 6×5 is 5 more than 5×5; 6×8 is double 3×8; or $9 \times 7 = (10 \times 7) - 7$. In solving division facts, students often think of the related multiplication fact. So to solve $64 \div 8$, a student might use his or her knowledge of the related multiplication fact, $8 \times 8 = 64$.

In grade 4, division continues to be a focal point as it relates to "Developing quick recall of multiplication facts and related division facts and fluency with whole number multiplication." To be "fluent" means to be able to perform a function readily and effortlessly. Fluency is built on well-understood relationships involving numbers and operations with numbers. "Quick recall" is an aspect of fluency, and means that students can give a quick response to a basic fact without using inefficient means. For example, students who have quick recall for the fact 8×7 should not have to add $7 + 7 + 7 + 7 + 7 + 7 + 7$ to arrive at the answer. Students in grade 4 should continue to apply thinking strategies to acquire basic facts, eventually resulting in instant or quick recall of those facts. They apply that quick recall of basic multiplication and division facts to develop fluency with multidigit multiplication and begin initial work with multidigit division.

In grade 5, division becomes a focal point again as it relates to "Developing an understanding of and fluency with division of whole numbers." Although students should learn efficient procedures to solve division problems such as the standard division algorithm, students' fluency with multidigit division develops as they apply their understanding of models for division, place value, properties, and the relationship of division to multiplication. For example, to solve the division problem $300 \div 12$, a student might think in the following way:

I know 12× 20 is 240. That leaves 60 left (300 − 240).
I know 12 × 5 = 60. So I have 12 groups of 20 and
12 groups of 5, or 25 groups total. So 360 ÷12 = 25.

In solving the problem, the student used the distributive property of multiplication over addition and the partial products of 12×20 and 12×5. Relating the partial products strategy to the standard algorithm can help students understand why the standard algorithm works and help them use the standard algorithm more efficiently and without errors.

$$
\begin{array}{r}
25 \\
12\overline{)300} \\
-24 \quad \rightarrow 12 \times 20 = 240 \\
\overline{60} \\
-60 \quad \rightarrow 12 \times 5 = 60 \\
\overline{0}
\end{array}
$$

Standard division algorithm $300 \div 12$ highlighting the partial products of 12×20 and 12×5

Another student might solve this same problem by breaking the 300 into the partial quotients of 240 and 60 and thinking 240/12 + 60/12. One might also use the distributive property of multiplication over subtraction: 300/12 = 360/12 – 60/12. As students' work with fractions and ratios develops, students might also solve the problem by simplifying: 300/12 = 100/4 = 25/1.

Students' work with estimation and mental mathematics can help them judge the reasonableness of their answer when using the standard division algorithm. For example, in solving 453 ÷ 62, a student might estimate that the answer will be close to 7, since 60 × 7 = 420 and 60 × 8 = 480. Another student might determine that the quotient will be a single-digit number, since 62 × 10 is 620.

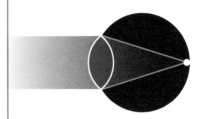

DEVELOPMENT-OF-FRACTIONS TASK: *How does the topic of fractions develop as students progress from grade 3 through grade 5? What are other core topics in grades 3–5, and how do these topics develop as students move from grade 3 through grade 5? NCTM's* Curriculum Focal Points for Prekindergarten through Grade 8 Mathematics *and the supporting grade-level books, NCTM's* Navigations series *books, and your own curriculum documents are good references to use in this exercise.*

Focusing the Curriculum You Teach

Now that you have taken some time to think about learning progressions and how students' knowledge can grow and deepen over time, the next step is to look at your curriculum and begin to organize it into more coherent instruction at each grade level. This task may seem daunting, but the intent is to use your existing curriculum as a starting point. States and districts may revise future curriculum documents on the basis of the framework provided by NCTM's *Curriculum Focal Points;* however, in the short term, you can use the Focal Points to prioritize topics of emphasis listed at each grade level in your current state and local curricula. A sample state curriculum for grade 4 is provided in Appendix D to show you an example of a curriculum that is organized around focal points (identified as "Big Ideas"). Use the questions in the Evaluating-My-Curriculum Task below to begin to evaluate your curriculum by highlighting focal areas and connections, as well as by identifying content that might be moved to other grades or areas that seem to be repeated year after year. You might want to use different colored highlighter markers to distinguish your focal areas and connections.

> A sample state curriculum for grade 4 is provided in Appendix D to show you an example of a curriculum that is organized around focal points.

EVALUATING-MY-CURRICULUM TASK: *Using your own curriculum for grades 3–5 and NCTM's Focal Points (see Appendixes A, B, and C), address the following questions:*

- *Do I think I currently have a focused mathematics curriculum in grades 3–5? Why or Why not?*

- *What important ideas or learning progressions can be seen in our existing mathematics curriculum at each grade level? Do any important ideas appear in NCTM's set of focal points that do not appear somewhere in our curriculum, and vice versa? If so, how do we address that discrepancy?*

- *Does our sequence of important ideas make sense mathematically? Does it connect logically with the mathematics in earlier and later grade levels and build from grade to grade without unnecessary repetition? If not, how can we change this sequencing?*

- *Can we tell from our own curriculum what topics will receive the most emphasis and how these topics are treated differently in grades 3, 4, and 5? How much time would you propose be spent on these areas of emphasis, and should that time be dispersed throughout the year or concentrated?*

- *What content areas or topics in our existing curriculum can we think of as "connections" with the identified foundational ideas or focal points? Can we better connect these areas with the main areas of emphasis instead of teaching them as separate topics?*

- *In general, what changes can be made to our curriculum, both overall and within the grades 3–5 band, to make it more focused?*

- *What concerns do I have about the idea of a focused mathematics curriculum in grades 3–5?*

Sample Responses to "Questions to Reflect On"

What are some of the major learning progressions that occur in grades 3–5?

Concepts and skills for multiplication and division are a major learning progression in grades 3–5. This progression begins in grade 3 with the development of the understanding of the meanings of multiplication and division and strategies to learn the basic multiplication and division facts. In grade 4, students should develop quick recall of the basic multiplication and division facts and begin to develop fluency with whole-number multiplication as well as do initial work with multidigit division. In grade 5, students should develop fluency with multidigit division.

Another major learning progression in grades 3–5 is the understanding of fractions. In grade 3, students should develop an understanding of the meaning of fractions and fraction equivalence. In grade 4, students connect their understanding of fractions with decimals. In grade 5, students develop fluency with the addition and subtraction of fractions and decimals.

In grades 3–5, students also progress in their understanding of geometric shapes and in developing measurement constructs as they relate to these shapes. In grade 3, the focus is on two-dimensional shapes and connections are made with perimeter as a measurable attribute. Students' knowledge deepens in grade 4 as they develop an understanding of area to measure two-dimensional shapes and regions. In grade 5, students work with three-dimensional shapes. Building on the introduction of area in grade 4, formulas for the area of a triangle, a parallelogram, and a trapezoid are developed and are used among other ways to find the surface areas of some solids. Volume is introduced in a way similar to the introduction of area for rectangles, and then extended to some more general solids such as rectangular and triangular prisms.

Algebra readiness is also developed in grades 3–5, particularly alongside work with Number and Operations as students develop understanding of properties of multiplication and division. Students also begin to use algebraic expressions to represent such measurement constructs as perimeter, area, and volume during work with two and three-dimensional shapes.

Appendix F of this book links specific activities from NCTM's Navigations series of with the Focal Points identified at each grade level. Grade-level books related to the Focal Points will also be produced for grades 3, 4, and 5 and will serve as important resources for teachers as well.

> Appendix F of this book links specific activities from NCTM's Navigations series of with the Focal Points.

How are basic facts and algorithms addressed in a focused curriculum?

Many of the Focal Points in grades 3–5 relate to the content strand of Number and Operations, so needless to say, basic facts and fluent use of algorithms (or procedures) to solve computational problems are important. However, it is crucially important that facts and procedures be learned with understanding. Instruction in basic facts should emphasize thinking strategies, and students should first develop understanding of the meanings of multiplication and division before quick recall is expected. Students should develop fluency with efficient procedures for multidigit multiplication and division problems, including the standard algorithm for each of these operations; however, these skills should always be developed alongside conceptual understanding. Focusing on why the procedures work using place-value concepts and properties of operations is needed so students gain facility with the use of these procedures. For example, the standard algorithm to multiply multidigit numbers begins to make more sense to students if they understand the use of the distributive property.

Standard Algorithm	Use of the Distributive Property
18	$10 + 8$
$\times 7$	$\times 7$
56	56 (7×8)
70	70 (7×10)
126	126
	OR $18 \cdot 7 = (10+8)7 = 10\cdot7 + 8\cdot7 = 70 + 56 = 126.$

Instruction to Support a Focused Curriculum

Questions to Reflect On

- What does instruction that supports depth of understanding and connections among mathematical ideas "look like"?
- How can questioning be used to support the development of depth of understanding and connections in a focused curriculum?
- What is the role of practice in a focused curriculum?
- What impact does instruction that supports a focused curriculum have on time management?

Effective mathematics teaching requires understanding what students know and need to learn and then challenging and supporting them to learn it well.

—The Teaching Principle,
Principles and Standards for School Mathematics

Although NCTM's Curriculum Focal Points can help prioritize and organize mathematics content, teachers and the instruction they provide are crucial to using focal points to improve student learning. Focusing mathematics around a few central ideas at each grade requires skilled teachers who know the content well and can connect mathematical ideas and teach for depth of understanding.

Use of the Process Standards

It is essential that teachers incorporate the Process Standards of Problem Solving, Reasoning and Proof, Communication, Connections, and Representation as described in *Principles and Standards for School Mathematics* (NCTM 200) into classroom instruction. Teachers should create a climate that supports mathematical thinking and communication. In this kind of classroom, students are accustomed to reasoning about a mathematical problem and justifying or explaining their results, representing mathematical ideas in multiple ways, and building new knowledge as well as applying knowledge through problem solving. Brief descriptions of the Process Standards can be found in the table below. More detailed descriptions can be found in *Principles and Standards for School Mathematics*.

NCTM Process Standards

Problem Solving. Through problem solving, students can not only apply the knowledge and skills they have acquired but can also learn new mathematical content. Problem solving is not a specific skill to be taught, but should permeate all aspects of learning. Teachers should make an effort to choose "good" problems—ones that invite exploration of an important mathematical concept and allow students the chance to solidify and extend their knowledge. Compare the two versions of a perimeter-and-area task below; whereas Task 1 requires students to do little more than correctly apply formulas, Task 2 engages them intellectually because it challenges them to search for something and is not imediately solvable. The instructional strategies used in the classroom should also promote collaborative problem solving. Students' learning of mathematics is enhanced in a learning environment that is a community of people collaborating to make sense of mathematical ideas (Hiebert et al. 1997).

Task 1
Find the area and perimeter of each rectangle:

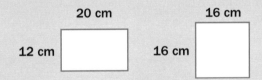

Task 2
Suppose you had 64 meters of fence with which you were going to build a pen for your large dog, Bones. What are some different sized and shaped pens you can make if you use all the fencing? What does the pen with the least play space look like? What is the biggest pen you can make—the one that allows Bones the most play space? Which pen size would be best for running?

Source: *Mathematics Teaching Today, Second Edition* (NCTM, 2007a, p. 36). Reprinted with permission.

Reasoning and Proof. For students to learn mathematics with understanding, it must make sense to them. Teachers can help students make sense of the mathematics they are learning by encouraging them to always explain and justify their solutions and strategies as well as evaluate other students' ideas. Questions such as "Why?" and "How do you know?" should be a regular part of classroom discussions. The teacher should respond in ways that focus on thinking and reasoning rather than only on getting the correct answer. Incorrect answers should not simply be judged wrong. Instead, teachers can help students identify the parts of their thinking that may be correct, often leading to new ideas and solutions that are correct.

Communication. Reasoning and Proof goes hand in hand with the process of Communication. Students should have plenty of opportunities and support for speaking, writing, reading, and listening in the mathematics classroom. Communicating one's ideas orally and in writing helps to solidify and refine learning. Listening to others' explanations can also sharpen learning by providing multiple ways to think about a problem. The teacher plays an important role in developing students' communication skills by modeling effective oral and written communication of mathematical ideas as well as giving students regular opportunities to communicate mathematically.

Connections. As students move through the grades, they should be presented with new mathematical content. Students' abilities to understand these new ideas depends greatly on connecting them with previously learned ideas. Mathematics is an integrated field of study and should be presented in this way instead of as a set of disconnected and isolated concepts and skills. Instruction should emphasize the interconnectedness of mathematical ideas and should be presented in a variety of contexts.

Representation. Mathematical ideas can be represented in a variety of ways: pictures, concrete materials, tables, graphs, numerical and alphabetical symbols, spreadsheet displays, and so on. Such representations should be an essential part of learning and doing mathematics and serve as a tool for thinking about and solving problems. Teachers should model representing mathematical ideas in a variety of ways and discuss why some representations are more effective than others in particular situations.

Facilitating Classroom Discourse

The Process Standards, especially the Communication Standard and the Reasoning and Proof Standard, are related to the discourse in the mathematics classroom. "The discourse of a classroom—the way of representing, thinking, talking, agreeing, and disagreeing—is central to what and how students learn mathematics" (NCTM 2007a, p. 46). The teacher plays an important role in initiating and facilitating this discourse and can do so in the following ways:

- posing questions and tasks that elicit, engage, and challenge each student's thinking;

- listening carefully to students' ideas and deciding what to pursue in depth from among the ideas that students generate during a discussion;

- asking students to clarify and justify their ideas orally and in writing and by accepting a variety of presentation modes;

- deciding when and how to attach mathematical notation and language to students' ideas:

- encouraging and accepting the use of multiple representations;

- making available tools for exploration and analysis;

- deciding when to provide information, when to clarify an issue, when to model, when to lead, and when to let students wrestle with a difficulty; and

- monitoring students' participation in discussions and deciding when and how to encourage each student to participate. (NCTM, 2007a, p. 45)

The following classroom vignette illustrates a teacher's use of effectively facilitating discourse in the mathematics classroom. In this discussion, a conjecture has been made by some students that the larger a number is, the more factors it has.

Vignette
Drawing on Mathematical Knowledge during Exploration Activities

Although the class period is nearing its end, the teacher invites one group to present to the rest of the class their conjecture that the larger the number, the more factors it has. She suggests that the students record the conjecture in their notebooks and discuss it in class tomorrow. Pausing for a moment before she sends them out to recess, she decides to provoke their thinking a bit more: "That's an interesting conjecture. Let's just think about it for a second. How many factors does, say, 3 have?"

"Two," call out several students.

"What are they?" she probes. "Yes, Deng?"

Deng quickly replies, "1 and 3."

"Let's try another one," continues the teacher. "What about 20?"

After a moment, several hands shoot up. She pauses to allow students to think, and asks, "Natasha?"

"Six: 1 and 20, 2 and 10, 4 and 5," answers Natasha with confidence.

The teacher suggests a couple more numbers, 9 and 15. She is conscious of trying to use only numbers that fit the conjecture. With satisfaction, she notes that most of the students are quickly able to produce all the factors for each of the numbers she gives them. Some used paper and pencil, some used calculators, and some used a combination of both. As she looks up at the clock, one child asks, "But what about 17? It doesn't seem to work."

"That's one of the things that you could examine for tomorrow. I want all of you to see if you can find out whether this conjecture always holds."

"I don't think it'll work for odd numbers," says one child.

"Check into it," smiles the teacher. "We'll discuss it tomorrow."

The teacher deliberately decides to leave the question unanswered. She wants to encourage students to persevere and to not expect her to provide all the answers.

Source: *Mathematics Teaching Today* (NCTM 2007a, p. 23). Reprinted with permission.

Use of Questioning to Focus Learning and Promote Connections

As described in the Introduction and the "Focusing Curriculum" section of this guide, using focal points to organize instruction does not mean teaching less or more content, but instead means directing the majority of your instruction at a smaller number of core areas with the goal of students' gaining a deeper mathematical understanding of those mathematical ideas and the connections among them. To teach for depth of understanding, teachers need to understand what their students are thinking and be able to support and extend that thinking. A teacher's use of questioning plays a vital role in focusing learning on foundational mathematical ideas and promoting mathematical connections. Such reasoning questions as "Why?" and "How do you know that?" posed during a lesson are great starters, but teachers also need to incorporate questioning techniques into their planning by thinking about specific questions to ask related to the particular topic. When planning instruction, teachers must also anticipate the kinds of answers they might get from students in response to questions posed.

Let us look at the following classroom example related to the grade-3 focal point of "Developing an understanding of fractions and fraction equivalence" to show a teacher's use of questioning to focus learning on essential ideas and promote connections.

> A teacher's use of questioning plays a vital role in focusing learning on foundational mathematical ideas and promoting mathematical connections.

Teacher: Suppose there are two groups of students trying to divide brownies equally among themselves. In the first group, there are 3 brownies being shared by 4 students, and in the second group, there are 6 brownies being shared by 8 people. Do the students in each group get the same amount of brownie?

Student: No, the group with 4 people get more because there's only 4 students and 3 brownies, but 8 people only get to share 6 brownies.

Teacher: Can you make a picture or drawing to show me this situation?

Group 1: 3 brownies shared
by 4 people

Group 2: 6 brownies shared
by 8 people

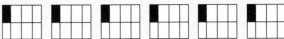

Teacher: Do the people in Group 1 get the same amount as the people in Group 2?

Student: Yes.

Teacher: But, it looks like to me that the students in Group 1 got 3 pieces of brownie and the students in Group 2 got 6 pieces of brownie each.

Student: But the second group's brownie was divided into more pieces, and 2 of their pieces equal the same amount as one of the other group's pieces.

Teacher: Can you describe the amount of brownie that each person in Group 1 got as a fraction?

Student: 1 out of the four pieces, so 1/4.

Teacher: So each person got 1/4 of each of the three brownies? So how many 1/4's did each person get in the first group altogether?

Student: Each person got 3/4's.

Teacher: What about the second group? What fraction represents the amount of brownie that each person got?

Student: 1/8.

Teacher: OK, so each person got one of the eight pieces, or 1/8, from each brownie. And there's 6 brownies altogether, so each person got how many eighths of a brownie.

Student: 6/8

Teacher: OK, so Group 1 got 3/4 of a brownie each and Group 2 got 6/8 of a brownie each. But, as you said, that's the same amount, since two of Group's 2 pieces can be combined to equal the same amount as Group 1's pieces. So we know now that 3/4 is the same as, or equivalent to, 6/8.

Another student's approach to this same problem might go something like this:

Student 2: The students in Group 2 each get the same amount as in Group 1 because even though there's twice as many people in Group 2, there's also twice as many brownies. So the first four people in the group can share 3 of the brownies and the second four people in the group can share the other 3 brownies just like in Group 1.

Teacher: What an interesting way to look at the problem. You're right. Thinking in that same way, suppose we had 12 people instead of 8 in the second group, how many brownies would they have to share to get the same amount as the students in Group 1?

Student 2: That would be an additional 4 people, so you'd need an additional 3 brownies, or 9 brownies total.

Teacher: Let's put this information in a table to keep track of what we've done and see if we notice any patterns.

Student 2: OK.

In this classroom example, rather than just respond to the incorrect answer from the first student, the teacher uses questions to guide the student in further thinking. By first asking the student to represent the problem with a picture, the student begins to visualize the problem better and correct his or her thinking. While the student can see in the visual representation that each student gets the same amount of brownie, the teachers guides the student into expressing the amounts as fractions and begins to help focus on the foundational idea of fraction equivalence.

The second student is stumbling on the idea of proportions and has made a great discovery. Although formal instruction with proportionality and the multiplicative nature of proportions is a focal point in later grades, the teacher leads the student's thinking further in this idea by proposing the involvement of 12 people instead of 8 and by suggesting that the student represent the various scenarios in a table. In so doing, in addition to focusing the discussion on the foundational idea of fraction equivalence, the teacher is also promoting connections with future content.

Students must learn mathematics with understanding, actively building new knowledge from experience and prior knowledge.

—The Learning Principle,
Principles and Standards for School Mathematics

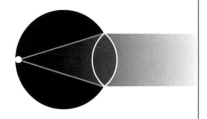

QUESTIONING TASK: *Below are a few different classroom assignments that might be given to students in grades 3–5. Identify any essential ideas that these activities address. Generate a list of questions that you might ask to focus students' attention on these ideas and to forge connections between important mathematical ideas.*

Sample Student Assignments

Student Assignment 1

Show all the rectangular regions you can make using 24 tiles (1-inch square). You need to use all the tiles. Count and keep a record of the area and perimeter of each rectangle and then look for and describe any relationships you notice.

Source: *Principles and Standards for School Mathematics* (Reston, Va.: NCTM, 2000, p. 183). Reprinted with permission.

Student Assignment 2

Which is more?
- 5/12 or 7/12 of a dozen doughnuts?
- 1/2 or 1/4 of a pie?
- 5/6 or 5/12 of a chocolate candy bar?
- 1/6 or 2/3 of a pizza?

Source: *Navigating through Number and Operations in Grades 3–5* (NCTM 2007b, pp. 34–35). Reprinted with permission.

Student Assignment 3

What is the value of the circle, triangle, and rectangle?

● + ▲ = 17

● + ▲ + ▬ = 26

▬ – ● = 4

Source: *Figure This!* CD-ROM (Reston, Va.: NCTM 2004, Challenge 58). Reprinted with permission.

CORRECTING-STUDENT-ERROR TASK: *A student incorrectly added the decimals in the figure below. What questioning or other techniques would you use to help the student correct his or her thinking?*

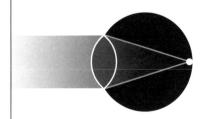

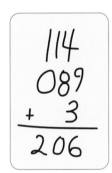

$$\begin{array}{r} 114 \\ 089 \\ +\ \ 3 \\ \hline 206 \end{array}$$

Jaron's group's incorrect solution to
1.14 g + .089 g + .3 g

Source: *Principles and Standards for School Mathematics* (NCTM 2000, p. 195). Reprinted with permission.

DEVELOPING-DEPTH-OF-UNDERSTANDING TASK: *Choose a focus point for grade 3, 4, or 5, such as fractions and fraction equivalence or division of whole numbers. What kinds of activities might you do with your class to help students acquire depth of understanding?*

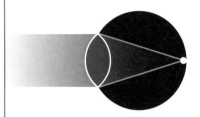

Sample Responses to "Questions to Reflect On"

What is the role of practice in a focused curriculum?

Practice of mathematical skills is necessary. For example, practice can help students become more confident and competent in using a computational procedure. Practice can also help commit facts to long-term memory, thereby freeing up working memory for more complex problems (National

Mathematics Advisory Panel 2007, slides 6-7). However, if students are mimicking a procedure without understanding the procedure and why it works, they often make mistakes, and the practice can solidify errors. Practice in a focused curriculum may also help connect previous learned foci with the current focal point areas. For example, when students are investigating the perimeters of two-dimensional figures in grade 3, they will also be practicing multidigit addition at the same time.

What impact does instruction that supports a focused curriculum have on time management?

Probably the phrase that is heard most from teachers (and rightly so) is "I don't have enough time…" whether it is in reference to planning, teaching, or assessing. However, the focal points model is designed to have a positive impact on teachers' time. By reorganizing curriculum into key focus areas, the result will be less repetition and reteaching and more time for rigorous and in-depth study of important mathematics at each grade level. An important consideration for teachers to think about is *quality of time* and how they might use their time differently both in planning and during instruction. Instead of teaching "a skill a day," teachers need to have a more holistic plan for instruction. Teachers might think about "What essential understandings and connections do I want my students to have?" and "What sequence of lessons will I use to promote these understandings and connections?" as they plan for instruction. Teachers will need to spend time thinking carefully about what examples and problems they will chose to support a mathematical concept and what questions they will ask to focus student thinking as well as to address anticipated student responses. In the end, however, this time spent up-front by teachers in planning should pay off during instruction as well as assessment as students connect mathematical ideas and learn mathematics with a greater depth of understanding.

Teachers' Mathematical Knowledge and Professional Development

Questions to Reflect On

- What special knowledge of mathematics is needed by teachers to teach a focused curriculum?
- How can a culture of mathematics learning that supports teaching a focused curriculum be created?
- How can in-school and districtwide professional development be changed to improve teachers' mathematical knowledge?

Mathematical Knowledge Needed by Teachers

Besides knowing students and instructional practices to support learning, teachers need a strong knowledge of the mathematics content themselves. However, what specific knowledge of mathematics is needed to teach mathematics, especially at the elementary school level? Shulman introduced the term *pedagogical content knowledge,* which he claimed went beyond a knowledge of subject matter to subject-matter knowledge needed for teaching (Shulman 1986). Such knowledge includes a variety of special mathematics teaching skills, for example—

- knowing which concepts are typically difficult for students and how to address those difficulties;

- being able to select and model effective representations for mathematical ideas;

- selecting good problems;

- examining students' work and being able to pinpoint and analyze sources of errors;

- being flexible in thinking about alternative ways to solve a problem as described by students;

- assessing students in order to make important instructional decisions related to the content, such as when to provide additional instruction or when to move on; and

- deciding which student ideas to call attention to during class discussions.

All these teaching tasks require a special kind of mathematical knowledge that is more than just knowing the mathematics for oneself.

Another resource about the knowledge needed for teaching is Liping Ma's book *Knowing and Teaching Elementary Mathematics* (Ma 1999). In her study, Ma compared Chinese and U.S. elementary school teachers' mathematical knowledge. Even having only 11 to 12 years of formal schooling versus the 16 to 18 years of most U.S. teachers, most of the Chinese teachers had a solid knowledge of the mathematics they taught, and some had what she called a "profound understanding of fundamental mathematics." This foundation included not only the ability to explain the mathematics taught and the ability to make up problems to illustrate what needs to be learned but also having a broader view of elementary school mathematics, which involves knowing what students should know before teaching a topic and knowing how the topic fits into later mathematical learning. It is developed only after years of teaching, but we need to prepare our teachers with enough knowledge to enable them to use their knowledge of mathematics, of students, and of teaching students to grow through the years as some of the Chinese teachers did. Most of the Chinese teachers Ma interviewed had a connected and coherent knowledge of core mathematical ideas similar to what NCTM's

Focal Points advocate. Ma's work also contradicts the myth that "elementary mathematics is 'basic,' superficial, and commonly understood" (p. 146). Instead, elementary school mathematics can be quite intense and demanding, and it lays the important groundwork on which all future mathematics learning is based. Elementary school teachers must themselves possess a strong mathematical understanding of the underpinnings of elementary mathematics if they are to impart this wisdom to their students. Take some time to explore some of the classroom scenarios that are presented in Ma's book and to think about how you would handle these situations in your own classroom.

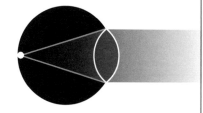

KNOWING AND TEACHING ELEMENTARY MATHEMATICS TASKS: *The following classroom scenarios were presented in* Knowing and Teaching Elementary Mathematics *(Ma 1999). Discuss how you would address these situations in your own classroom.*

Multidigit Multiplication Scenario

You notice that several of your students are making the same mistake as illustrated below in multidigit multiplication, that is, forgetting to "move the numbers" (i.e., the partial products) over on each line. How would you address this problem with your students?

$$
\begin{array}{r}
123 \\
\times\ 645 \\
\hline
615 \\
492 \\
738 \\
\hline
1845
\end{array}
$$

The Relationship-between-Perimeter-and-Area Scenario

Imagine that one of your students comes to class very excited. She tells you that she has figured out a theory that you never told the class. She explains that she has discovered that as a perimeter of a closed figure increases, the area also increases. She shows you this picture to prove what she is doing. How would you respond to this student?

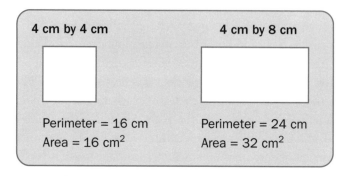

School Culture and Professional Development

Teaching a more focused curriculum at each grade level will be a major shift for most teachers and schools. Important considerations to remember are that these efforts will take time, and that collaboration among all parties involved is essential. A school culture must be developed that supports open discussions among teachers, instructional leaders, and administrators about how this outcome can be realized and what short- and long-term changes need to be made to implement the changes. Professional development must also include more emphasis on teachers' mathematical knowledge as well as pedagogical knowledge of how to teach that content in ways that promote a deeper understanding of the important mathematical ideas and connections. The identified focal points and connections at each grade level could be the basis for designing professional development activities to improve teachers' mathematical knowledge.

PROFESSIONAL DEVELOPMENT PLAN TASK: *Work with other teachers in your grade or across grades to create a professional development plan that will support teaching a focused curriculum. Identify both short- and long-term goals.*

> Professional development must also include more emphasis on teachers' mathematical knowledge as well as pedagogical knowledge of how to teach that content in ways that promote a deeper understanding of the important mathematical ideas and connections.

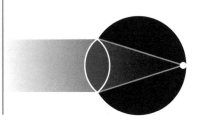

Assessment

Questions to Reflect On

- How do we measure the depth of understanding that a focused curriculum is meant to impart?
- How do we measure students' sophistication of strategies used to solve problems or their fluency with numbers?
- What is the role of classroom assessments in a focused curriculum?
- What role do state assessments play in a focused curriculum? In what ways might state assessments be changed to better promote a focused curriculum?

Focusing Assessment

How does having a more focused curriculum affect these kinds of assessments? Overall, if the curriculum is more focused at each grade level, then in turn, assessments should also be more focused and should attempt to monitor and measure students' progress through these core areas. In addition, if

Assessment should support the learning of important mathematics and furnish useful information to both teachers and students.

—*Principles and Standards for School Mathematics*

Assessments must also measure the level or depth of students' understanding rather than simply ascertain whether the correct answer was given.

---

the main goal of a focused curriculum is to develop depth of understanding, assessments must also measure the level or depth of students' understanding rather than simply ascertain whether the correct answer was given. Consider the grade–5 Focal Point of "Developing an understanding of and fluency with division of whole numbers." Although dividing whole numbers is a specific skill that we want students to have, it means a lot more than being able to mimic the steps of the long-division algorithm. This Focal Point includes many other components of developing understanding and fluency, such as understanding models of division, estimating quotients, choosing the best way to solve a problem (for instance, by paper and pencil or by mental calculation), understanding why a procedure like the standard algorithm works, deciding when to use division to solve a problem, and interpreting the remainder.

Measuring Depth of Understanding

Open-ended questioning and tasks often yield more insight into students' understanding and thinking than problems for which only an answer—without justification or reasoning—is expected. Such open-ended problems usually ask students to explain their thinking, show their work, or otherwise provide more information than just an answer.

Let us look at a sample problem and sample responses from students to show different levels of understanding related to fractions and fraction equivalence.

> José ate 1/2 of a pizza.
> Ella ate 1/2 of another pizza.
> José said that he ate more pizza than Ella, but Ella said they both ate the same amount.
> Use words and pictures to show that José could be right.

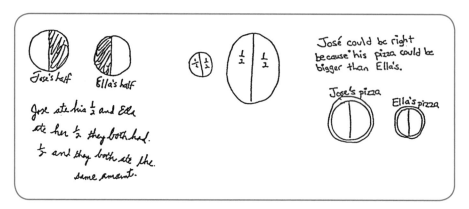

Student responses to the "pizza" problem (Dossey, Mullis, and Jones 1993)
Source: *Principles and Standards for School Mathematics* (NCTM 2000, p. 199). Reprinted with permission.

The first student seemed to draw two pizzas that were exactly the same and divided each in half. In this instance, the two halves of pizza are the same size, since the relative whole for each pizza is the same size. This student seems to have an initial understanding of fractions to represent parts of wholes. However, whether this student understands that the size of a fractional part is relative to the whole is not clear. The student was not able to show how José could eat more pizza than Ella even if both ate half of a pizza. The teacher might probe this student's thinking further by drawing different sized pizzas and discussing how the halves compare. The second student correctly drew two different-sized pizzas showing that half of one pizza is larger than half of the other pizza. This student seems to understand that the size of a fractional part is relative to the whole; however, the teacher might ask the student to verbally or in writing explain his or her thinking further, since only a picture was given with no explanation to go with the picture. The third student included written words and drawings to correctly show how José could have eaten more even though both ate half of a pizza. This student clearly communicates that the size of a fraction is relative to the size of the whole.

Even problems that clearly have only one correct answer can be made more open-ended by asking students to justify or explain their answer. Sometimes students will give the correct answer, but their reasoning may reveal misconceptions and lack of true understanding. Consider the following sample problem and two students' responses:

Which is larger, 0.6 or 0.53? How do you know?

Student 1:   "0.53 is larger, since 53 is larger than 6."

Student 2:   "0.6 is larger, since hundredths are smaller than tenths."

The first student gives an incorrect answer, and his or her explanation shows that the student does not understand the place value of decimals. Although the second student gives the correct answer, his or her explanation is incomplete, and whether the student really understands the place-value concepts related to decimals is unclear. The student may be overgeneralizing the fact that the more places to the right of the decimal, the smaller the individual place value gets. Therefore, he or she may reason that 0.6 is larger than 0.53 because it does not have a digit in the hundredths place, the smaller place value. The teacher could determine whether the student is using this flawed reasoning by asking which is larger, 0.95 or 0.4. If the reply is 0.4, then although the student understands that the value of each place gets smaller as you move to the right of the decimal, he or she seems not to be looking at the overall value of the number as a whole (NCTM 2005, p. 202). However, if the student does give the correct answer, again saying that 0.95 is larger, then the student's original (correct) explanation was correct but not

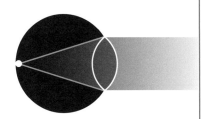

detailed and complete enough to show that he or she did understand. In the comparison of 0.6 and 0.53, this student may have reasoned that hundredths are smaller than tenths, so one needs only to look at the tenths place and see that 6 is larger than 5. Students sometimes struggle with giving clear explanations for their reasoning, so questioning them further is important to determine their level of understanding. Teachers can also help students give more complete explanations of their reasoning by helping them expand on their explanations and by modeling complete explanations.

SAMPLE-STUDENT-WORK TASK: *Evaluate the sample student work provided in Appendix F for depth of understanding.*

MEASURING DEPTH OF UNDERSTANDING TASK: *What might an assessment that tries to measure the depth and complexity of the division focal point for grade 5 or another focal point for grade 3, 4, or 5 look like? Develop a sample assessment task related to this focal point that you might give to students.*

Classroom Assessment versus Large-Scale Assessment

Daily classroom assessment is crucial to a focused curriculum and to the goal of having students' knowledge deepen over time. Teachers gather assessment information from a variety of sources, such as classroom observations, students' responses to questions and classroom discussions, daily classroom work, homework, performance tasks, student journals, portfolios of sample work, quizzes, and tests. The kinds of classroom assessments will not likely change, but the focal points and connections identified for a particular grade should be used to help teachers narrow in on what they want to assess. Those focal points should be at the forefront of a teacher's mind when planning instruction and assessments. Teachers must also analyze their students' level of understanding and fluency or sophistication in solving problems, and plan their instruction with the goal of advancing students' understanding.

Although large-scale assessments like state tests can provide such useful data as comparing students' learning in a whole content area, these tests do not always furnish an accurate view of students' depth of understanding. Often, these tests are written to measure a very specific skill, for example, the ability to multiply a two-digit number by a two-digit number. Currently, these tests also attempt to measure a broad range of topics, resulting in teachers' not being able to spend enough time developing students' depth of understanding. As states change their curriculum to be more focused at each grade level, state assessments should change as well. In the short term, teachers will have to balance the requirements of their state tests with organizing their instruction to promote important areas of emphasis and a greater depth of understanding.

> The identified focal points and connections identified for a particular grade should be used to help teachers narrow in on what they want to assess.

Concluding Thoughts

NCTM's *Curriculum Focal Points for Prekindergarten through Grade 8 Mathematics: A Quest for Coherence* was written as a framework to guide states and school districts as they design and organize the next revisions of their expectations, standards, curricula, and assessment programs. The goal of this guide is to expand on those ideas and provide a professional development tool to help individual teachers and groups of teachers begin to think about what a focused curriculum means and how they might begin to build some focus into their existing curriculum. By focusing more intensely on fewer topics at each grade level, students should gain a deeper understanding of mathematical ideas that will continue to grow and become more sophisticated as they move through the grades. As you work through your own professional development plan to build focus into your curriculum and teaching over the year, take time to revisit the "Questions to Reflect On" at the beginning of each section as well as some of the professional development tasks presented throughout this guide. In what ways has your instruction become more focused? What changes have you seen in the level of understanding of your students? What additional goals do you have for bringing focus to your curriculum and instruction?

Appendix A

Curriculum Focal Points and Connections for Grade 3

The set of three curriculum focal points and related connections for mathematics in grade 3 follow. These topics are the recommended content emphases for this grade level. It is essential that these focal points be addressed in contexts that promote problem solving, reasoning, communication, making connections, and designing and analyzing representations.

Grade 3 Curriculum Focal Points	Connections to the Focal Points
Number and Operations and Algebra: **Developing understandings of multiplication and division and strategies for basic multiplication facts and related division facts** Students understand the meanings of multiplication and division of whole numbers through the use of representations (e.g., equal-sized groups, arrays, area models, and equal "jumps" on number lines for multiplication, and successive subtraction, partitioning, and sharing for division). They use properties of addition and multiplication (e.g., commutativity, associativity, and the distributive property) to multiply whole numbers and apply increasingly sophisticated strategies based on these properties to solve multiplication and division problems involving basic facts. By comparing a variety of solution strategies, students relate multiplication and division as inverse operations.	***Algebra:*** Understanding properties of multiplication and the relationship between multiplication and division is a part of algebra readiness that develops at grade 3. The creation and analysis of patterns and relationships involving multiplication and division should occur at this grade level. Students build a foundation for later understanding of functional relationships by describing relationships in context with such statements as, "The number of legs is 4 times the number of chairs."
Number and Operations: **Developing an understanding of fractions and fraction equivalence** Students develop an understanding of the meanings and uses of fractions to represent parts of a whole, parts of a set, or points or distances on a number line. They understand that the size of a fractional part is relative to the size of the whole, and they use fractions to represent numbers that are equal to, less than, or greater than 1. They solve problems that involve comparing and ordering fractions by using models, benchmark fractions, or common numerators or denominators. They understand and use models, including the number line, to identify equivalent fractions.	***Measurement:*** Students in grade 3 strengthen their understanding of fractions as they confront problems in linear measurement that call for more precision than the whole unit allowed them in their work in grade 2. They develop their facility in measuring with fractional parts of linear units. Students develop measurement concepts and skills through experiences in analyzing attributes and properties of two-dimensional objects. They form an understanding of perimeter as a measurable attribute and select appropriate units, strategies, and tools to solve problems involving perimeter. ***Data Analysis:*** Addition, subtraction, multiplication, and division of whole numbers come into play as students construct and analyze frequency tables, bar graphs, picture graphs, and line plots and use them to solve problems.
Geometry: **Describing and analyzing properties of two-dimensional shapes** Students describe, analyze, compare, and classify two-dimensional shapes by their sides and angles and connect these attributes to definitions of shapes. Students investigate, describe, and reason about decomposing, combining, and transforming polygons to make other polygons. Through building, drawing, and analyzing two-dimensional shapes, students understand attributes and properties of two-dimensional space and the use of those attributes and properties in solving problems, including applications involving congruence and symmetry.	***Number and Operations:*** Building on their work in grade 2, students extend their understanding of place value to numbers up to 10,000 in various contexts. Students also apply this understanding to the task of representing numbers in different equivalent forms (e.g., expanded notation). They develop their understanding of numbers by building their facility with mental computation (addition and subtraction in special cases, such as 2,500 + 6,000 and 9,000 − 5,000), by using computational estimation, and by performing paper-and-pencil computations.

Source: Reprinted from *Curriculum Focal Points for Prekindergarten through Grade 8: A Quest for Coherence* (Reston, Va.: National Council of Teachers of Mathematics, 2006), p. 15. Used with permission.

Appendix B
Curriculum Focal Points and Connections for Grade 4

The set of three curriculum focal points and related connections for mathematics in grade 4 follow. These topics are the recommended content emphases for this grade level. It is essential that these focal points be addressed in contexts that promote problem solving, reasoning, communication, making connections, and designing and analyzing representations.

Grade 4 Curriculum Focal Points	Connections to the Focal Points
Number and Operations and Algebra: Developing quick recall of multiplication facts and related division facts and fluency with whole number multiplication Students use understandings of multiplication to develop quick recall of the basic multiplication facts and related division facts. They apply their understanding of models for multiplication (i.e., equal-sized groups, arrays, area models, equal intervals on the number line), place value, and properties of operations (in particular, the distributive property) as they develop, discuss, and use efficient, accurate, and generalizable methods to multiply multidigit whole numbers. They select appropriate methods and apply them accurately to estimate products or calculate them mentally, depending on the context and numbers involved. They develop fluency with efficient procedures, including the standard algorithm, for multiplying whole numbers, understand why the procedures work (on the basis of place value and properties of operations), and use them to solve problems.	*Algebra:* Students continue identifying, describing, and extending numeric patterns involving all operations and nonnumeric growing or repeating patterns. Through these experiences, they develop an understanding of the use of a rule to describe a sequence of numbers or objects. *Geometry:* Students extend their understanding of properties of two-dimensional shapes as they find the areas of polygons. They build on their earlier work with symmetry and congruence in grade 3 to encompass transformations, including those that produce line and rotational symmetry. By using transformations to design and analyze simple tilings and tessellations, students deepen their understanding of two-dimensional space.
Number and Operations: Developing an understanding of decimals, including the connections between fractions and decimals Students understand decimal notation as an extension of the base-ten system of writing whole numbers that is useful for representing more numbers, including numbers between 0 and 1, between 1 and 2, and so on. Students relate their understanding of fractions to reading and writing decimals that are greater than or less than 1, identifying equivalent decimals, comparing and ordering decimals, and estimating decimal or fractional amounts in problem solving. They connect equivalent fractions and decimals by comparing models to symbols and locating equivalent symbols on the number line.	*Measurement:* As part of understanding two-dimensional shapes, students measure and classify angles. *Data Analysis:* Students continue to use tools from grade 3, solving problems by making frequency tables, bar graphs, picture graphs, and line plots. They apply their understanding of place value to develop and use stem-and-leaf plots.
Measurement: Developing an understanding of area and determining the areas of two-dimensional shapes Students recognize area as an attribute of two-dimensional regions. They learn that they can quantify area by finding the total number of same-sized units of area that cover the shape without gaps or overlaps. They understand that a square that is 1 unit on a side is the standard unit for measuring area. They select appropriate units, strategies (e.g., decomposing shapes), and tools for solving problems that involve estimating or measuring area. Students connect area measure to the area model that they have used to represent multiplication, and they use this connection to justify the formula for the area of a rectangle.	*Number and Operations:* Building on their work in grade 3, students extend their understanding of place value and ways of representing numbers to 100,000 in various contexts. They use estimation in determining the relative sizes of amounts or distances. Students develop understandings of strategies for multidigit division by using models that represent division as the inverse of multiplication, as partitioning, or as successive subtraction. By working with decimals, students extend their ability to recognize equivalent fractions. Students' earlier work in grade 3 with models of fractions and multiplication and division facts supports their understanding of techniques for generating equivalent fractions and simplifying fractions.

Source: Reprinted from *Curriculum Focal Points for Prekindergarten through Grade 8: A Quest for Coherence* (Reston, Va.: National Council of Teachers of Mathematics, 2006), p. 16. Used with permission.

Appendix C
Curriculum Focal Points and Connections for Grade 5

The set of three curriculum focal points and related connections for mathematics in grade 5 follow. These topics are the recommended content emphases for this grade level. It is essential that these focal points be addressed in contexts that promote problem solving, reasoning, communication, making connections, and designing and analyzing representations.

Grade 5 Curriculum Focal Points	Connections to the Focal Points
Number and Operations and Algebra: Developing an understanding of and fluency with division of whole numbers Students apply their understanding of models for division, place value, properties, and the relationship of division to multiplication as they develop, discuss, and use efficient, accurate, and generalizable procedures to find quotients involving multidigit dividends. They select appropriate methods and apply them accurately to estimate quotients or calculate them mentally, depending on the context and numbers involved. They develop fluency with efficient procedures, including the standard algorithm, for dividing whole numbers, understand why the procedures work (on the basis of place value and properties of operations), and use them to solve problems. They consider the context in which a problem is situated to select the most useful form of the quotient for the solution, and they interpret it appropriately.	*Algebra:* Students use patterns, models, and relationships as contexts for writing and solving simple equations and inequalities. They create graphs of simple equations. They explore prime and composite numbers and discover concepts related to the addition and subtraction of fractions as they use factors and multiples, including applications of common factors and common multiples. They develop an understanding of the order of operations and use it for all operations. *Measurement:* Students' experiences connect their work with solids and volume to their earlier work with capacity and weight or mass. They solve problems that require attention to both approximation and precision of measurement. *Data Analysis:* Students apply their understanding of whole numbers, fractions, and decimals as they construct and analyze double-bar and line graphs and use ordered pairs on coordinate grids. *Number and Operations:* Building on their work in grade 4, students extend their understanding of place value to numbers through millions and millionths in various contexts. They apply what they know about multiplication of whole numbers to larger numbers. Students also explore contexts that they can describe with negative numbers (e.g., situations of owing money or measuring elevations above and below sea level.)
Number and Operations: Developing an understanding of and fluency with addition and subtraction of fractions and decimals Students apply their understandings of fractions and fraction models to represent the addition and subtraction of fractions with unlike denominators as equivalent calculations with like denominators. They apply their understandings of decimal models, place value, and properties to add and subtract decimals. They develop fluency with standard procedures for adding and subtracting fractions and decimals. They make reasonable estimates of fraction and decimal sums and differences. Students add and subtract fractions and decimals to solve problems, including problems involving measurement.	
Geometry and Measurement and Algebra: Describing three-dimensional shapes and analyzing their properties, including volume and surface area Students relate two-dimensional shapes to three-dimensional shapes and analyze properties of poly-hedral solids, describing them by the number of edges, faces, or vertices as well as the types of faces. Students recognize volume as an attribute of three-dimensional space. They understand that they can quantify volume by finding the total number of same-sized units of volume that they need to fill the space without gaps or overlaps. They understand that a cube that is 1 unit on an edge is the standard unit for measuring volume. They select appropriate units, strategies, and tools for solving problems that involve estimating or measuring volume. They decompose three-dimensional shapes and find surface areas and volumes of prisms. As they work with surface area, they find and justify relationships among the formulas for the areas of different polygons. They measure necessary attributes of shapes to use area formulas to solve problems.	

Source: Reprinted from *Curriculum Focal Points for Prekindergarten through Grade 8: A Quest for Coherence* (Reston, Va.: National Council of Teachers of Mathematics, 2006), p. 17. Used with permission.

Appendix D

Sample State Curriculum for Grade 4 Organized around Focal Points

K-8 MATHEMATICS STANDARDS
GRADE 4

BIG IDEA 1: *Develop quick recall of multiplication facts and related division facts and fluency with whole number multiplication.*	
BENCHMARK CODE	**BENCHMARK**
MA.4.A.1.1	Use and describe various models for multiplication in problem-solving situations, and demonstrate recall of basic multiplication and related division facts with ease.
MA.4.A.1.2	Multiply multi-digit whole numbers through four digits fluently, demonstrating understanding of the standard algorithm, and checking for reasonableness of results, including solving real-world problems.

Access Points for Students with Significant Cognitive Disabilities		
Independent:	*Supported:*	*Participatory:*
MA.4.A.1.In.a Solve problems involving combining (multiplying) or separating into (dividing) equal sets with quantities to 30 using objects and pictures with numerals. MA.4.A.1.In.b Recall addition facts with sums to 18 and related subtraction facts. MA.4.A.1.In.c Solve real-world addition and subtraction problems with two-digit numbers to 30 without regrouping, and check for accuracy. MA.4.A.1.In.d Use properties such as the commutative and additive identity as strategies to solve addition problems.	MA.4.A.1.Su.a Identify the meaning of the +, −, and = signs. MA.4.A.1.Su.b Solve addition facts with sums to 12 and related subtraction facts using numerals with sets of pictures and the +, −, and = signs. MA.4.A.1.Su.c Solve real-world problems involving addition facts with sums to 12 and related subtraction facts.	MA.4.A.1.Pa.a Recognize when items have been added to and removed from groups of objects in daily activities. MA.4.A.1.Pa.b Continue in a familiar routine with the addition or removal of a familiar person, action, or object in three or more settings.

Source: Reprinted by permission of the publisher from *2007 Florida Sunshine State Standards for Mathematics* (Tallahassee, Fla.: Florida Department of Education, 2007), page 42.

Sample State Curriculum for Grade 4
Organized around Focal Points—*Continued*

K-8 MATHEMATICS STANDARDS
GRADE 4

BIG IDEA 2: *Develop an understanding of decimals, including the connection between fractions and decimals.*	
BENCHMARK CODE	**BENCHMARK**
MA.4.A.2.1	Use decimals through the thousandths place to name numbers between whole numbers.
MA.4.A.2.2	Describe decimals as an extension of the base-ten number system.
MA.4.A.2.3	Relate equivalent fractions and decimals with and without models, including locations on a number line.
MA.4.A.2.4	Compare and order decimals, and estimate fraction and decimal amounts in real-world problems.

Access Points for Students with Significant Cognitive Disabilities		
Independent:	*Supported:*	*Participatory:*
MA.4.A.2.In.a Apply the concepts of counting, grouping, and place value with whole numbers to create sets of tens and ones to identify the value of whole numbers to 50. MA.4.A.2.In.b Identify differences between halves, fourths, and a whole. MA.4.A.2.In.c Express and represent fractions, including halves and fourths, as parts of a whole and parts of a set using objects, pictures, and number names.	MA.4.A.2.Su.a Apply the concept of grouping to create sets of tens and ones to 18 as a strategy for counting objects. MA.4.A.2.Su.b Identify half as a part of a whole.	MA.4.A.2.Pa.a Communicate desire for more in one routine or familiar activity. MA.4.A.2.Pa.b Communicate desire for none in a routine or familiar activity. MA.4.A.2.Pa.c Indicate desire for less in routines. MA.4.A.2.Pa.d Imitate counting two or more objects or actions in multiple activities. MA.4.A.2.Pa.e Match one object to a like object or picture using one-to-one correspondence.

Source: Reprinted by permission of the publisher from *2007 Florida Sunshine State Standards for Mathematics* (Tallahassee, Fla.: Florida Department of Education, 2007), page 43.

(Continued)

Sample State Curriculum for Grade 4
Organized around Focal Points—*Continued*

K-8 MATHEMATICS STANDARDS
GRADE 4

BIG IDEA 3: *Develop an understanding of area and determine the area of two-dimensional shapes.*	
BENCHMARK CODE	**BENCHMARK**
MA.4.G.3.1	Describe and determine area as the number of same-sized units that cover a region in the plane, recognizing that a unit square is the standard unit for measuring area.
MA.4.G.3.2	Justify the formula for the area of the rectangle "area = base x height."
MA.4.G.3.3	Select and use appropriate units, both customary and metric, strategies, and measuring tools to estimate and solve real-world area problems.

Access Points for Students with Significant Cognitive Disabilities		
Independent:	*Supported:*	*Participatory:*
MA.4.G.3.In.a Identify examples of the distance around all sides (perimeter) and area of squares and rectangles in the environment. MA.4.G.3.In.b Find the area of rectangular and square objects using square units. MA.4.G.3.In.c Measure whole inches and feet using a ruler to solve real-world linear measurement problems. MA.4.G.3.In.d Identify time to the quarter hour using a clock. MA.4.G.3.In.e Identify the date and month using a calendar. MA.4.G.3.In.f Measure weight using whole pounds and capacity using whole cups to solve real-world problems.	MA.4.G.3.Su.a Identify examples of area in the environment. MA.4.G.3.Su.b Measure length of objects using whole inches. MA.4.G.3.Su.c Identify the capacity of containers as holds more or holds less. MA.4.G.3.Su.d Identify a clock as a tool to tell time. MA.4.G.3.Su.e Identify months using a calendar.	MA.4.G.3.Pa.a Identify similarities in the size of two or more familiar objects in daily activities. MA.4.G.3.Pa.b Identify similarities in shape of familiar objects in daily activities. MA.4.G.3.Pa.c Follow two or more directional instructions in routines or activities. MA.4.G.3.Pa.d Indicate two or more locations of preferred objects or activities within the learning environment.

Source: Reprinted by permission of the publisher from *2007 Florida Sunshine State Standards for Mathematics* (Tallahassee, Fla.: Florida Department of Education, 2007), page 44.

Sample State Curriculum for Grade 4
Organized around Focal Points—*Continued*

K-8 MATHEMATICS STANDARDS
GRADE 4

SUPPORTING IDEAS	
Algebra	
BENCHMARK CODE	**BENCHMARK**
MA.4.A.4.1	Generate algebraic rules and use all four operations to describe patterns, including nonnumeric growing or repeating patterns.
MA.4.A.4.2	Describe mathematics relationships using expressions, equations, and visual representations.
MA.4.A.4.3	Recognize and write algebraic expressions for functions with two operations.

Access Points for Students with Significant Cognitive Disabilities		
Independent:	*Supported:*	*Participatory:*
MA.4.A.4.In.a Identify and extend growing visual and number patterns.	MA.4.A.4.Su.a Identify and copy two-element repeating visual patterns using objects and pictures.	MA.4.A.4.Pa.a Identify items that belong together to complete a set in routines or activities.
MA.4.A.4.In.b Describe equal and unequal sets using terms including greater than, less than, and equal to.	MA.4.A.4.Su.b Determine if the number in two sets of objects to 10 are same or different (equal or unequal).	MA.4.A.4.Pa.b Follow a two-element repeating pattern in two or more routines, activities, or settings.
MA.4.A.4.In.c Identify the rule, including 1 less, 2 less, and 3 less, represented in number pairs.	MA.4.A.4.Su.c Use the rule 1 more to identify the next number with numbers 1 to 20.	MA.4.A.4.Pa.c Indicate the next step in a familiar sequence of an activity.
		MA.4.A.4.Pa.d Indicate the end of a familiar sequence of an activity.

Source: Reprinted by permission of the publisher from *2007 Florida Sunshine State Standards for Mathematics* (Tallahassee, Fla.: Florida Department of Education, 2007), page 45.

(Continued)

Sample State Curriculum for Grade 4
Organized around Focal Points—*Continued*

K-8 MATHEMATICS STANDARDS
GRADE 4

SUPPORTING IDEAS	
Geometry and Measurement	
BENCHMARK CODE	**BENCHMARK**
MA.4.G.5.1	Classify angles of two-dimensional shapes using benchmark angles (i.e. 45?, 90?, 180?, and 360?).
MA.4.G.5.2	Identify and describe the results of translations, reflections, and rotations of 45, 90, 180, 270, and 360 degrees, including figures with line and rotational symmetry.
MA.4.G.5.3	Identify and build a three-dimensional object from a two-dimensional representation of that object and vice versa.

Access Points for Students with Significant Cognitive Disabilities		
Independent:	*Supported:*	*Participatory:*
MA.4.G.5.In.a Locate angles in two-dimensional shapes including triangles and rectangles. MA.4.G.5.In.b Identify examples of two-dimensional figures that are the same shape and size (congruency) and figures that are visually the same on both sides of a central dividing line (symmetry) in the environment. MA.4.G.5.In.c Sort three-dimensional objects, such as cubes, cylinders, cones, rectangular prisms, and spheres.	MA.4.G.5.Su.a Locate angles within a triangle. MA.4.G.5.Su.b Identify two-dimensional figures that are visually the same on both sides of a central dividing line (symmetry). MA.4.G.5.Su.c Match three-dimensional objects with models, such as a cube, cylinder, cone, and sphere.	MA.4.G.5.Pa.a Identify differences in familiar objects with two-dimensional shapes, such as circle, square, or triangle. MA.4.G.5.Pa.b Identify two or more familiar three-dimensional objects in daily activities. MA.4.G.5.Pa.c Identify objects, pictures, or symbols associated with two or more activities in the daily schedule.

Source: Reprinted by permission of the publisher from *2007 Florida Sunshine State Standards for Mathematics* (Tallahassee, Fla.: Florida Department of Education, 2007), page 46.

Sample State Curriculum for Grade 4
Organized around Focal Points—*Continued*

K-8 MATHEMATICS STANDARDS
GRADE 4

SUPPORTING IDEAS	
Number and Operations	
BENCHMARK CODE	**BENCHMARK**
MA.4.A.6.1	Use and represent numbers through millions in various contexts, including estimation of relative sizes of amounts or distances.
MA.4.A.6.2	Use models to represent division as: • the inverse of multiplication • as partitioning • as successive subtraction
MA.4.A.6.3	Generate equivalent fractions and simplify fractions.
MA.4.A.6.4	Determine factors and multiples for specified whole numbers.
MA.4.A.6.5	Relate halves, fourths, tenths, and hundredths to decimals and percents.
MA.4.A.6.6	Estimate and describe reasonableness of estimates; determine the appropriateness of an estimate versus an exact answer.

Access Points for Students with Significant Cognitive Disabilities		
Independent:	*Supported:*	*Participatory:*
MA.4.A.6.In.a Express, represent, and use whole numbers 0 to 50 in various contexts, including money. MA.4.A.6.In.b Compare and order whole numbers to 50 using pictures or tallies and a number line. MA.4.A.6.In.c Use the inverse relationship of addition and subtraction as a strategy to solve problems. MA.4.A.6.In.d Use skip counting by 5s and 10s to determine amounts to 50. MA.4.A.6.In.e Use strategies such as comparing and grouping to estimate quantities to 10.	MA.4.A.6.Su.a Express, represent, and use whole numbers to 18 using sets of objects and pictures, number names, and numerals in various contexts, including money. MA.4.A.6.Su.b Count, compare, and order numbers 0 to 18 using sets of objects and pictures with numerals MA.4.A.6.Su.c Use objects and pictures to represent the relationship between addition and subtraction facts. MA.4.A.6.Su.d Use ordinal numbers, including first and second, in real-world situations.	MA.4.A.6.Pa.a Respond to a prompt to identify a specified part of an object. MA.4.A.6.Pa.b Solve problems by selecting a preferred or necessary item from two or more options in a routine.

Source: Reprinted by permission of the publisher from *2007 Florida Sunshine State Standards for Mathematics* (Tallahassee, Fla.: Florida Department of Education, 2007), page 47.

35

Appendix E

A Roadmap to the NCTM Navigations Series from the Grades 3, 4, and 5 Curriculum Focal Points

Developing and implementing a program of instruction for grades 3–5 calls for a wide variety of resources. One resource that offers curriculum planners and teachers special assistance is the Navigations series published by the National Council of Teachers of Mathematics. Each book in this popular series provides teachers with ideas and suggestions for presenting essential, Standards-based content through lively hands-on activities for students. A CD-ROM, filled with rich supplemental ideas for teachers and students alike, accompanies each volume. The books expand on and illustrate the vision of mathematics instruction outlined in NCTM's *Principles and Standards for School Mathematics* (2000), a landmark publication that identifies six principles that form the foundation of any high-quality program of mathematics instruction: Equity, Curriculum, Teaching, Learning, Assessment, and Technology.

NCTM's recently released *Curriculum Focal Points for Prekindergarten through Grade 8 Mathematics: A Quest for Coherence* (2000), demonstrates how schools can apply the Curriculum Principle in prekindergarten through grade 8. Already recognized as an influential force in curriculum development across the country, *Curriculum Focal Points* identifies important mathematical topics for each grade level, prekindergarten through grade 8, and encapsulates them in a set of Focal Points that can serve to organize curriculum design and instruction at and across grade levels.

Curriculum Focal Points   Grade 3

Number and Operations and Algebra: Developing understandings of multiplication and division and strategies for basic multiplication facts and related division facts

Students understand the meanings of multiplication and division of whole numbers through the use of representations (e.g., equal-sized groups, arrays, area models, and equal "jumps" on number lines for multiplication, and successive subtraction, partitioning, and sharing for division). They use properties of addition and multiplication (e.g., commutativity, associativity, and the distributive property) to multiply whole numbers and apply increasingly sophisticated strategies based on these properties to solve multiplication and division problems involving basic facts. By comparing a variety of solution strategies, students relate multiplication and division as inverse operations.

Navigating through Number and Operations in Grades 3–5 (Duncan, Natalie N., Charles Geer, DeAnn Huinker, Larry Leutizinger, Ed Rathmell, and Charles Thompson, edited by Francis (Skip) Fennell, 2007; NCTM stock number 12952)

Overview	Introduction (pages 1–12), Chapter 1 (pages 13–14), Chapter 2 (pages 49–51), Chapter 3 (pages 91–93), Chapter 4 (pages 121–22)
Equal Groups	"Two Types of Multiplication Problems" (pages 52–61)
Basic Operations	"Two Types of Division Problems" (pages 62–71)
Arrays	"Splitting Arrays" (pages 72–79) "Learning Multiplication Facts with Arrays" (pages 108–13)
Basic Facts	"A Problem-solving Approach to Basic Facts" (pages 94–103) "Building on Known Facts" (pages 114–16)
Computation	"'Make Ten' to Multiply" (pages 104–8)
Inverse Operations	"To Divide, Think 'Multiplication'" (pages 117–20)
Distributive Property	"Summing Partial Products to Multiply" (pages 128–33)
Decomposing	"Using Mental Mathematics to Divide" (pages 134–40)

Number and Operations: Developing an understanding of fractions and fraction equivalence

Students develop an understanding of the meanings and uses of fractions to represent parts of a whole, parts of a set, or points or distances on a number line. They understand that the size of a fractional part is relative to the size of the whole, and they use fractions to represent numbers that are equal to, less than, or greater than 1. They solve problems that involve comparing and ordering fractions by using models, benchmark fractions, or common numerators or denominators. They understand and use models, including the number line, to identify equivalent fractions.

Navigating through Number and Operations in Grades 3–5 (Duncan, Natalie N., Charles Geer, DeAnn Huinker, Larry Leutizinger, Ed Rathmell, and Charles Thompson, edited by Francis (Skip) Fennell, 2007; NCTM stock number 12952)

Fraction Concept	"Fraction Models" (pages 27–33)
Equivalence	"Actions on Fractions" (pages 34–40)

Geometry: Describing and analyzing properties of two-dimensional shapes

Students describe, analyze, compare, and classify two-dimensional shapes by their sides and angles and connect these attributes to definitions of shapes. Students investigate, describe, and reason about decomposing, combining, and transforming polygons to make other polygons. Through building, drawing, and analyzing two-dimensional shapes, students understand attributes and properties of two-dimensional space and the use of those attributes and properties in solving problems, including applications involving congruence and symmetry.

Navigating through Geometry in Grades 3–5 (Gavin, M. Katherine, Louise P. Belkin, Ann Marie Spinelli, Judy St. Marie, edited by Gilbert J. Cuevas, 2001; NCTM stock number 12173)

Overview	Introduction (pages 1–8), Chapter 1 (pages 9–10), Chapter 2 (pages 35–36), Chapter 3 (pages 47–48), Chapter 4 (pages 75–76)
Basic Shapes	"Build What I Created" (pages 11–14)
Triangle Properties	"Thinking about Triangles" (pages 15–21)
Quadrilaterals	"Roping in Quadrilaterals" (pages 22–25)
Attributes of Solids	"Building Solids" (pages 26–30)
Symmetry	"Patchwork Symmetry" (pages 49–52)
Transformations	"Tetrominoes Cover-Up" (pages 59–63) "Motion Commotion" (pages 64–67)
Manipulating Shapes	"Puzzles with Pizzazz" (pages 77–79)

Connections to Curriculum Focal Points — Grade 3

Navigating through Number and Operations in Grades 3–5 (Duncan, Natalie N., Charles Geer, DeAnn Huinker, Larry Leutizinger, Ed Rathmell, and Charles Thompson, edited by Francis (Skip) Fennell, 2007; NCTM stock number 12952)

Inverse Operations	"Adding Up to Subtract" (pages 123–27)

Navigating through Algebra in Grades 3–5 (Cuevas, Gilbert J., and Karol Yeatts, edited by Gilbert J. Cuevas, 2001; NCTM stock number 753)

Patterns	"Hundred-Board Wonders" (pages 9–11) "Calculator Patterns" (pages 15–17)
Formula Development	"Watch Them Grow" (pages 12–14)
Graphing	"Graphic Stories" (pages 31–32)
Variables	"The Variable Machine" (pages 39–40)
Equality	"Algebra Scales" (pages 44–47)

Navigating through Geometry in Grades 3–5 (Gavin, M. Katherine, Louise P. Belkin, Ann Marie Spinelli, Judy St. Marie, edited by Gilbert J. Cuevas, 2001; NCTM stock number 12173)

Shapes	"Thinking about Triangles" (pages 15–22)
Classifying	"Roping in Quadrilaterals" (pages 23–25)
Symmetry	"Patchwork Symmetry" (pages 49–51)
Covering	"Tetrominoes Cover-Up" (pages 59–63)

Navigating through Measurement in Grades 3–5 (Anderson, Nancy Canavan, M. Katherine Gavin, Judith Dailey, Walter Stone, and Janice Vuolo, edited by Gilbert J. Cuevas, 2005; NCTM stock number 12525)

Perimeter	"Ants' Picnic" (pages 24–27)

Navigating through Problem Solving and Reasoning in Grade 3 (Yeatts, Karol L., Michael T. Battista, Sally Mayberry, Denisse R. Thompson, and Judith S, Zawojewsky, edited by Bonnie H. Litwiller, 2004; NCTM stock number 12719)

Overview	Introduction (pages 1–6)
Number Relationships	"Walking into Place Value" (pages 8–11)
Algebraic Reasoning	"And We All Go Marching" (pages 12–18)
Decomposing Polygons	"Cut It Apart, Put It Together" (pages 19–25)
Measurement	"How Many Are Too Many?" (pages 26–30)

Curriculum Focal Points   Grade 4

Number and Operations and Algebra: Developing quick recall of multiplication facts and related division facts and fluency with whole number multiplication.

Students use understandings of multiplication to develop quick recall of the basic multiplication facts and related division facts. They apply their understanding of models for multiplication (i.e., equal sized groups, arrays, area models, equal intervals on the number line), place value, and properties of operations (in particular, the distributive property) as they develop, discuss, and use efficient, accurate, and generalizable methods to multiply multidigit whole numbers. They select appropriate methods and apply them accurately to estimate products or calculate them mentally, depending on the context and numbers involved. They develop fluency with efficient procedures, including the standard algorithm, for multiplying whole numbers, understand why the procedures work (on the basis of place value and properties of operations), and use them to solve problems.

Navigating through Number and Operations in Grades 3–5 (Duncan, Natalie N., Charles Geer, DeAnn Huinker, Larry Leutizinger, Ed Rathmell, and Charles Thompson, edited by Francis (Skip) Fennell, 2007; NCTM stock number 12952)

Overview	Introduction (pages 1–11), Chapter 1 (pages 13–14), Chapter 2 (pages 49–51), Chapter 3 (pages 91–93), Chapter 4 (pages 121–22)
Equal-Sized Groups	"Two Types of Multiplication Problems" (pages 52–61)
Partitioning and Sharing	"Two Types of Division Problems" (pages 62–71)
Arrays	"Splitting Arrays" (pages 72–79) "Learning Multiplication Facts with Arrays" (pages 108–13)
Fact Acquisition	"A Problem-Solving Approach to Basic Facts" (pages 94–03)
Estimation	" 'Make Ten' to Multiply" (pages 104–7)
Division Facts	"To Divide, Think 'Multiplication' " (pages 117–20)
Distributive Property	"Summing Partial Products to Multiply" (pages 128–33)

| Mental Calculation | "Using Mental Math to Divide" (pages 134–40) |
| Strategies for Multiplication | "Going Over or Under to Estimate" (pages 141–46) |

Number and Operations: Developing an understanding of decimals, including the connections between fractions and decimals

Students understand decimal notation as an extension of the base-ten system of writing whole numbers that is useful for representing more numbers, including numbers between 0 and 1, between 1 and 2, and so on. Students relate their understanding of fractions to reading and writing decimals that are greater than or less than 1, identifying equivalent decimals, comparing and ordering decimals, and estimating decimal or fractional amounts in problem solving. They connect equivalent fractions and decimals by comparing models to symbols and locating equivalent symbols on the number line.

Navigating through Number and Operations in Grades 3–5 (Duncan, Natalie N., Charles Geer, DeAnn Huinker, Larry Leutizinger, Ed Rathmell, and Charles Thompson, edited by Francis (Skip) Fennell, 2007; NCTM stock number 12952)

Place Value	"Place Value in Whole Numbers and Decimals" (pages 15–21)
Models	"Fraction Models" (pages 27–33) "Taking an Hour for Clock Fractions" (pages 147–54)
Comparing and Ordering	"Actions on Fractions" (pages 34–40)
Representing Decimals	"Fractions with a Point" (pages 41–48)

Measurement: Develop an understanding of area and determining the areas of two-dimensional shapes

Students recognize area as an attribute of two-dimensional regions. They learn that they can quantify area by finding the total number of same-sized units of area that cover the shape without gaps or overlaps. They understand that a square that is 1 unit on a side is the standard unit for measuring area. They select appropriate units, strategies (e.g., decomposing shapes), and tools for solving problems that involve estimating or measuring area. Students connect area measure to the area model that they have used to represent multiplication, and they use this connection to justify the formula for the area of a rectangle.

Navigating through Measurement in Grades 3–5 (Anderson, Nancy Canavan, M. Katherine Gavin, Judith Dailey, Walter Stone, and Janice Vuolo, edited by Gilbert J. Cuevas, 2005; NCTM stock number 12525)

Covering	"Big Cover-Up" (pages 53–57)
Area of Rectangle	"Stuck on Stickers" (pages 58–61)
Decomposing	"Geo-Explorations—Parallelograms" (pages 66–74)
Surface Area	"Wrap It Up" (pages 83–88)

Navigating through Number and Operations in Grades 3–5 (Duncan, Natalie N., Charles Geer, DeAnn Huinker, Larry Leutizinger, Ed Rathmell, and Charles Thompson, edited by Francis (Skip) Fennell, 2007; NCTM stock number 12952)

| Area Model | "Number Name Discovery" (pages 22–26) |

Connections to Curriculum Focal Points

Grade 4

Navigating through Number and Operations in Grades 3–5 (Duncan, Natalie N., Charles Geer, DeAnn Huinker, Larry Leutizinger, Ed Rathmell, and Charles Thompson, edited by Francis (Skip) Fennell, 2007; NCTM stock number 12952)

Division Facts	"Two Types of Division Problems" (pages 62–71)
Basic Facts	"Building on Known Facts" (pages 114–16)
Basic Operations	"Adding Up to Subtract" (pages 123–27)

Navigating through Algebra in Grades 3–5 (Cuevas, Gilbert J., and Karol Yeatts, edited by Gilbert J. Cuevas, 2001; NCTM stock number 753)

Patterns	"Hundred-Board Wonders" (pages 9–11)
	"Calculator Patterns" (pages 15–17)
Formula Development	"Watch Them Grow" (pages 12–14)
Area Measure	"Tiling a Patio" (pages 18–22)
Change	"The Ups and Downs of Patterns" (pages 27–30)
Tables	"What's the Best Deal?" (pages 33–36)
Variables	"The Variable Machine" (pages 39–40)
Equality	"Algebra Scales" (pages 44–47)
Properties	"I Spy Patterns" (pages 48–50)
Functions	"Triangle Rule Machine" (pages 58–60)

Navigating through Measurement in Grades 3–5 (Anderson, Nancy Canavan, M. Katherine Gavin, Judith Dailey, Walter Stone, and Janice Vuolo, edited by Gilbert J. Cuevas, 2005; NCTM stock number 12525)

Attributes	"Measurement Madness" (pages 16–18)
Perimeter	"Ants Picnic" (pages 24–25)
Angle Measure	"Measurement Scavenger Hunt" (pages 34–38)

Navigating through Geometry in Grades 3–5 (Gavin, M. Katherine, Louise P. Belkin, Ann Marie Spinelli, and Judy St. Marie, edited by Gilbert J. Cuevas, 2001; NCTM stock number 12173)

Shapes	"Thinking about Triangles" (pages 15–22)
Classifying	"Roping in Quadrilaterals" (pages 23–25)
Symmetry	"Patchwork Symmetry" (pages 49–51)
Covering	"Tetrominoes Cover-Up" (pages 59–63)
Transformations	"Motion Commotion" (pages 64–68)
3-D	"Exploring Packages" (pages 80–82)

Navigating through Problem Solving and Reasoning in Grade 4 (Yeatts, Karol L., Michael T. Battista, Sally Mayberry, Denisse R. Thompson, and Judith S, Zawojewsky, edited by Bonnie H. Litwiller, 2005; NCTM stock number 12886)

Overview	Introduction (pages 1–6)
Number Sets	"Discovering Primes as the Ancient Mathematicians Did" (pages 8–13)
Geometric Properties	"Making and Investigating Puzzles" (pages 24–29)
Measurement	"Fascinating Measures" (pages 32–39)

Curriculum Focal Points   Grade 5

Number and Operations and Algebra: Developing an understanding of, and fluency with, division of whole numbers

Students apply their understanding of models for division, place value, properties, and the relationship of division to multiplication as they develop, discuss, and use efficient, accurate, and generalizable procedures to find quotients involving multidigit dividends. They select appropriate methods and apply them accurately to estimate quotients or calculate them mentally, depending on the context and numbers involved. They develop fluency with efficient procedures, including the standard algorithm, for dividing whole numbers, understand why the procedures work (on the basis of place value and properties of operations), and use them to solve problems. They consider the context in which a problem is situated to select the most useful form of the quotient for the solution, and they interpret it appropriately.

Navigating through Number and Operations in Grades 3–5 (Duncan, Natalie N., Charles Geer, DeAnn Huinker, Larry Leutizinger, Ed Rathmell, and Charles Thompson, edited by Francis (Skip) Fennell, 2007; NCTM stock number 12952)

Overview	Introduction (pages 1–11), Chapter 1 (pages 13–14), Chapter 2 (pages 49–51), Chapter 3 (pages 91–93), Chapter 4 (pages 121–22)
Partitioning and Sharing	"Two Types of Division Problems" (pages 62–71)
Fact Acquisition	"A Problem-Solving Approach to Basic Facts" (pages 94–103)
Division Facts	"To Divide, Think Multiplication" (pages 117–20)
Mental Calculation	"Using Mental Math to Divide" (pages 134–40)

Number and Operations: Developing an understanding of and fluency with addition and subtraction of fractions and decimals.

Students apply their understanding of fractions and fraction models to represent the addition and subtraction of fractions with unlike denominators as equivalent calculations with like denominators. They apply their understandings of decimal models, place value, and properties to add and subtract decimals. They develop fluency with standard procedures for adding and subtracting fractions and decimals. They make reasonable estimates of fraction and decimal sums and differences. Students add and subtract fractions and decimals to solve problems, including problems involving measurement.

Navigating through Number and Operations in Grades 3-5 (Duncan, Natalie N., Charles Geer, DeAnn Huinker, Larry Leutizinger, Ed Rathmell, and Charles Thompson, edited by Francis (Skip) Fennell, 2007; NCTM stock number 12952)

Computation	"Adding and Subtracting Common Fractions" (pages 80–85)
Models	"Taking an Hour for Clock Fractions" (pages 147–54)
Addition	"Taking an Hour for Clock Fractions" (pages 147–54)

Geometry and Measurement and Algebra: Describing three-dimensional shapes and analyzing their properties, including volume and surface area. Geometry and Measurement and Algebra: Describing three-dimensional shapes and analyzing their properties, including volume and surface area.

Students relate two-dimensional shapes to three-dimensional shapes and analyze properties of polyhedral solids, describing them by the number of edges, faces, or vertices as well as the types of faces. Students recognize volume as an attribute of three-dimensional space. They understand that they can quantify volume by finding the total number of same-sized units of volume that they need to fill the space without gaps or overlaps. They understand that a cube that is 1 unit on an edge is the standard unit for measuring volume. They select appropriate units, strategies, and tools for solving problems that involve estimating or measuring volume. They decompose three-dimensional shapes and find surface areas and volumes of prisms. As they work with surface area, they find and justify relationships among the formulas for the areas of different polygons. They measure necessary attributes of shapes to use area formulas to solve problems.

Navigating through Measurement in Grades 3–5 (Anderson, Nancy Canavan, M. Katherine Gavin, Judith Dailey, Walter Stone, and Janice Vuolo, edited by Gilbert J. Cuevas, 2005; NCTM stock number 12525)

Overview	Introduction (pages 1–8), Chapter 1 (pages 11–12), Chapter 2 (pages 29–30), Chapter 3 (pages 51–52), Chapter 4 (pages 75–76)
Volume	"Building Boxes" (pages 77–82)
Surface Area	"Wrap It Up!" (pages 83–88)

Navigating through Geometry in Grades 3–5 (Gavin, M. Katherine, Louise P. Belkin, Ann Marie Spinelli, and Judy St. Marie, edited by Gilbert J. Cuevas, 2001; NCTM stock number 12173)

Overview	Introduction (pages 1–7), Chapter 1 (pages 9–10), Chapter 2 (pages 35–36), Chapter 3 (pages 47–48), Chapter 4 (pages 75–76)
Solids	"It's the View That Counts" (pages 86–87)

Connections to the Focal Points   Grade 5

Navigating through Number and Operations in Grades 3–5 (Duncan, Natalie N., Charles Geer, DeAnn Huinker, Larry Leutizinger, Ed Rathmell, and Charles Thompson, edited by Francis (Skip) Fennell, 2007; NCTM stock number 12952)

Number Classes	"Number Name Discoveries" (pages 22–26)

Navigating through Algebra in Grades 3-5 (Cuevas, Gilbert J., and Karol Yeatts, edited by Gilbert J. Cuevas, 2001; NCTM stock number 753)

Area Measure	"Tiling a Patio" (pages 18–22)
Systems of Equations	"Building Houses" (pages 51–53)
Areas	"Squares Cubed" (pages 64–66)

Navigating through Problem Solving and Reasoning in Grade 5 (Yeatts, Karol L., Michael T. Battista, Sally Mayberry, Denisse R. Thompson, and Judith S, Zawojewsky, edited by Bonnie H. Ltwiller, 2007; NCTM stock number 13012)

Overview	Introduction (pages 1–9)
Number	"PINs and Other Secret Codes" (pages 10–18)
Algebra	"Carina's Pet Shop" (pages 19–32)
3-D	"Making and Breaking Solids" (pages 33–44)

Appendix F: Sample Student Work

Comparison of 5/12 and 7/12

Sample Work 1

Which is more?

$\frac{5}{12}$ or $\boxed{\frac{7}{12}}$ of a dozen doughnuts?

How do you know?

$\boxed{\frac{5}{12}} > \boxed{\frac{7}{12}}$ because the denominators are the same. The denominators are 12, and 12. The numerators are 5 and 7. 5 is less than 7.

First you look at the denominators

Denominators — Whole #.
Numerator — Part of a whole #.

Steps —
● First look at denominators
● If the same look at the numerators and compare them.

$\boxed{\frac{5}{12}}$ $\boxed{\frac{7}{12}}$ $\frac{5}{12}$ $\boxed{\frac{7}{12}}$

Sample Work 2

Which is more?

$\frac{5}{12}$ or $\boxed{\frac{7}{12}}$ of a dozen doughnuts?

O = doughnuts

How do you know?

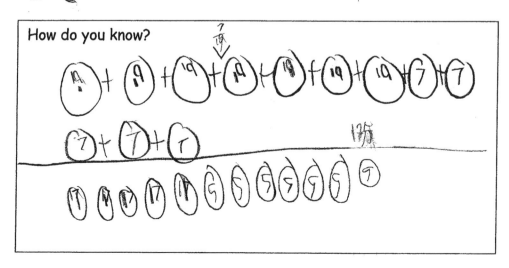

Comparison of 5/12 and 7/12 (*Continued*)

Sample Work 3

Which is more?

$\frac{5}{12}$ or $\frac{7}{12}$ of a dozen doughnuts?

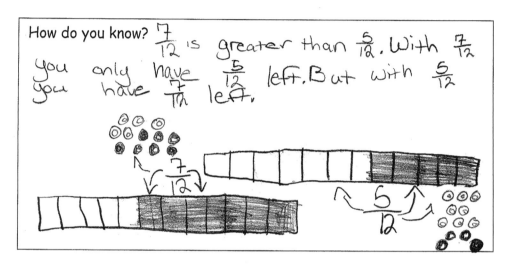

Sample Work 4

Which is more?

$\frac{5}{12}$ or $\frac{7}{12}$ of a dozen doughnuts?

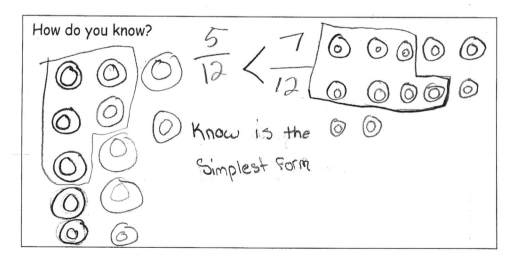

Comparison of 5/12 and 7/12—*Continued*

Sample Work 5

Which is more?

$\frac{5}{12}$ or $\frac{7}{12}$ of a dozen doughnuts? $\frac{7}{12}$

How do you know?

If you multiply by 2 for both numbers
you will get..... $\frac{7}{12}$ is greater than $\frac{5}{12}$

$$\frac{7 \times 2 \ 14}{12 \times 2 \ 24} > \frac{5 \times 10}{12 \times 24}$$

Comparison of 5/6 and 5/12—*Continued*

Sample Work 1

Which is more?

$\frac{5}{6}$ or $\frac{5}{12}$ of a chocolate candy bar?

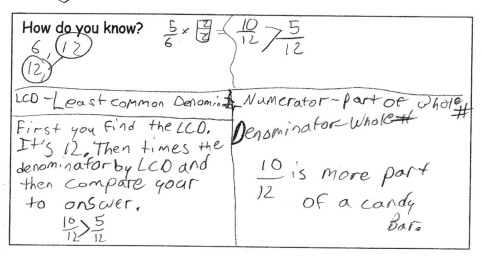

How do you know? $\frac{5}{6} \times \boxed{\frac{2}{2}} = \frac{10}{12} > \frac{5}{12}$

6, 12
12

LCD – Least common Denomin. Numerator – part of whole #

First you find the LCD. Denominator – Whole #
It's 12. Then times the
denominator by LCD and
then compare your $\frac{10}{12}$ is more part
to answer. of a candy
$\frac{10}{12} > \frac{5}{12}$ bar.

Sample Work 2

Which is more?

$\frac{5}{6}$ or $\frac{5}{12}$ of a chocolate candy bar?

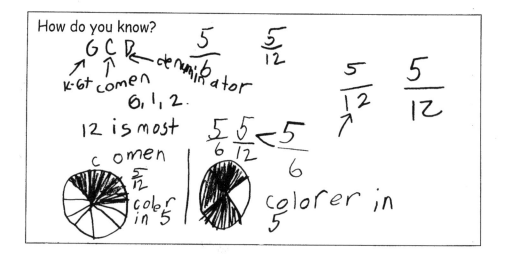

How do you know?

GCD ← denominator
K-Gt comen
6, 1, 2.

12 is most
comen $\frac{5}{6} \frac{5}{12} < \frac{5}{6}$
$\frac{5}{12}$ $\frac{5}{12}$ $\frac{5}{12}$
color
in 5 colorer in

Comparison of 5/6 and 5/12—*Continued*

Sample Work 3

Which is more?

$\frac{5}{6}$ or $\frac{5}{12}$ of a chocolate candy bar?

How do you know?

Sample Work 4

Which is more?

$\frac{5}{6}$ or $\frac{5}{12}$ of a chocolate candy bar?

How do you know?

Comparison of 1/6 and 2/3

Sample Work 1

Which is more?

$\frac{1}{6}$ or $\frac{2}{3}$ of a pizza?

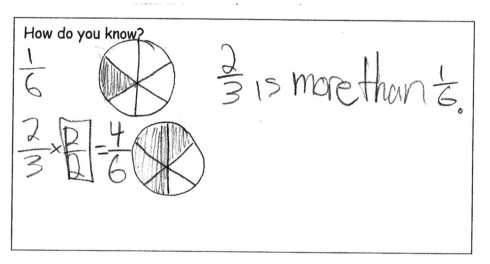

Sample Work 2

Which is more?

$\frac{1}{6}$ or $\frac{2}{3}$ of a pizza?

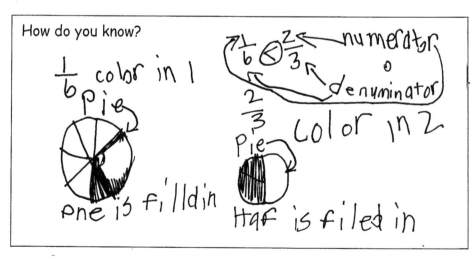

Comparison of 1/6 and 2/3—*Continued*

Sample Work 3

Which is more?

$\frac{1}{6}$ or $\frac{2}{3}$ of a pizza?

Sample Work 4

Which is more?

$\frac{1}{6}$ or $\frac{2}{3}$ of a pizza?

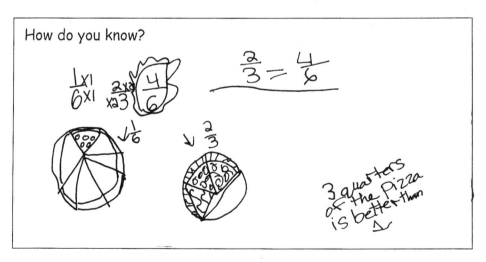

Find the Unknown Values

Sample Work 1

What is the value of the circle, triangle, and rectangle?

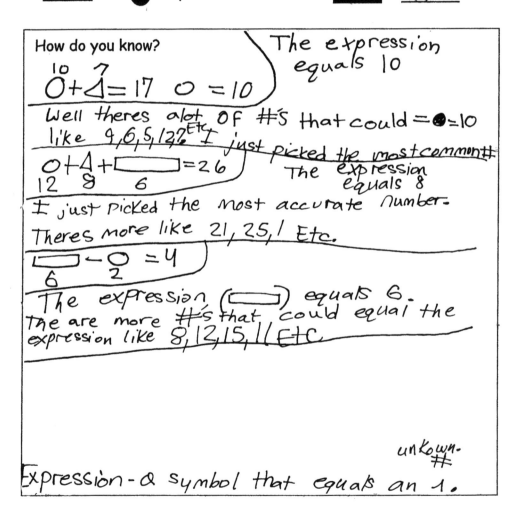

● + ▲ = 17   ● = _10_

● + ▲ + ▬ = 26   ▲ = _8_

▬ − ● = 4   ▬ = _6_

How do you know?

$\overset{10}{O} + \overset{7}{\triangle} = 17$ O = 10   ) The expression equals 10

Well theres alot of #'s that could = ●=10
like 9,6,5,12 Etc. I just picked the most common #

$\underset{12}{O} + \underset{8}{\triangle} + \underset{6}{\square} = 26$) The expression equals 8

I just picked the most accurate number.
Theres more like 21, 25, 1 Etc.

$\underset{6}{\square} − \underset{2}{O} = 4$)

The expression (▭) equals 6.
The are more #'s that could equal the
expression like 8, 12, 15, 11 Etc.

unkown-#

Expression - a symbol that equals an 1.

50

Find the Unknown Values—*Continued*

Sample Work 2

What is the value of the circle, triangle, and rectangle?

● + ▲ = 17

● = 13

● + ▲ + ▬ = 26

▲ = 4

▬ − ● = 4

▬ = 9

How do you know?

the ▬ is 9 because 17 + 9 = 26
and the ○ must be 13 because
9 − 13 = 4 so the △ must be 4 because
13 + 4 = 17

Find the Unknown Values—*Continued*

Sample Work 3

What is the value of the circle, triangle, and rectangle?

● + ▲ = 17

● + ▲ + ▬ = 26

▬ − ● = 4

● = $\underline{5}$

▲ = $\underline{12}$

▬ = $\underline{9}$

How do you know? How I got my answer was by subtracting 26 by 17 to figure out that the ▬ was 9. Then, I subtract 9 by 4 which told me that the ● was 5. The last thing I did was I subtract 17−5=12 to find out that the triangle which was the last shape was 12.

○+△=17 5+12=17

○+△+□=26 5+12+9=26

□−○=4 9−5=4

Find the Unknown Values—*Continued*

Sample Work 4

What is the value of the circle, triangle, and rectangle?

$\overset{5}{\bullet}$ + $\overset{12}{\blacktriangle}$ = 17 $\bullet$ = $\underline{5}$

$\overset{5}{\bullet}$ + $\overset{12}{\blacktriangle}$ + $\overset{9}{\blacksquare}$ = 26 $\blacktriangle$ = $\underline{12}$

$\overset{9}{\blacksquare}$ − $\overset{5}{\bullet}$ = 4 $\blacksquare$ = $\underline{9}$

How do you know?

I got it by trying out a lot of diffrent #'s un till one worked.

$17 - \bigcirc = \triangle \quad \triangle = 12$

$26 - \triangle - \bigcirc = \square \quad \square = 9$

$4 + \bigcirc = \square \quad \square = 9$

Appendix G

Task Sheets

Building-Focus Task

Think about your own grade level or one particular grade level. What are some of the essential mathematical ideas or topics that build a foundation for later learning? How do those mathematical ideas or topics connect to learning in later grades?

Development-of-Fractions Task

How does the topic of fractions develop as students progress from grade 3 through grade 5? What are other core topics in grades 3–5, and how do these topics develop as students move from grade 3 through grade 5? *NCTM's Curriculum Focal Points for Prekindergarten through Grade 8 Mathematics* and the supporting grade-level books, Navigations series books, and your own curriculum documents are good references to use in this exercise.

Evaluating-My-Curriculum Task

Using your own curriculum for grades 3–5 and NCTM's Focal Points, address the following questions:

1. Do I think I currently have a focused mathematics curriculum in grades 3–5? Why or why not?

2. What important ideas or learning progressions can be seen in our existing mathematics curriculum at each grade level? Do any important ideas appear in NCTM's set of focal points that do not appear somewhere in our curriculum, and vice versa? If so, how do we address that discrepancy?

3. Does our sequence of important ideas make sense mathematically? Does it connect logically with the mathematics in earlier and later grade levels and build from grade to grade without unnecessary repetition? If not, how can we change this sequencing?

4. Can we tell from our own curriculum what topics will receive the most emphasis and how these topics are treated differently in grades 3, 4, and 5? How much time would you propose be spent on these areas of emphasis, and should that time be dispersed throughout the year or concentrated?

5. What content areas or topics in our existing curriculum can we think of as "connections" with the identified important ideas or focal points? Can we better connect these areas with the main areas of emphasis instead of teaching them as separate topics?

6. In general, what changes can be made to our curriculum, both overall and within the grades 3–5 band, to make it more focused?

7. What concerns do I have about the idea of a focused mathematics curriculum in grades 3–5?

Questioning Task

The following are a few different classroom assignments that might be given to students in grades 3–5. Identify any essential ideas these activities address. Generate a list of questions that you might ask to focus students' attention on these important ideas and to forge connections among important mathematical ideas.

Student Assignment 1

Show all the rectangular regions you can make using 24 tiles (1-inch square). You need to use all the tiles. Count and keep a record of the area and perimeter of each rectangle, and then look for and describe any relationships you notice.

Essential Ideas   *Teacher Questions*

Student Assignment 2

Which is more?
- 5/12 or 7/12 of a dozen doughnuts?
- 1/2 or 1/4 of a pie?
- 5/6 or 5/12 of a chocolate candy bar?
- 1/6 or 2/3 of a pizza?

Essential Ideas   *Teacher Questions*

Student Assignment 3

What is the value of the circle, triangle, and rectangle?

● + ▲ = 17

● + ▲ + ▬ = 26

▬ − ● = 4

Essential Ideas   *Teacher Questions*

Correcting-Student-Error Task

A student incorrectly added the decimals in the figure below. What questioning or other techniques would you use to help the student correct his or her thinking?

Jaron's group's incorrect solution to
1.14 g + .089 g + .3 g

Developing-Depth-of-Understanding Task

Choose a focal point for grade 3, 4, or 5, for instance, fractions and fraction equivalence or division of whole numbers. What kinds of activities might you do with your class to help students acquire depth of understanding?

Sample-Student-Work Task

Evaluate the sample student work found in Appendix F for depth of understanding.

Knowing and Teaching Elementary School Mathematics Tasks

The following classroom scenarios were presented in Liping Ma's book *Knowing and Teaching Elementary Mathematics* (1999). Discuss how you would address these situations in your own classroom.

Multidigit-Multiplication Scenario

You notice that in multidigit multiplication, several of your students are making the same mistake illustrated below—forgetting to "move the numbers" (i.e., the partial products) over on each line. How would you address your students' difficulty with this problem?

$$
\begin{array}{r}
123 \\
\times\ 645 \\
\hline
615 \\
492 \\
738 \\
\hline
1845 \\
\end{array}
$$

Division-by-Fractions Scenario

Imagine that you are teaching division with fractions. To make this concept meaningful for children, many teachers relate mathematics to other things. Sometimes they try to come up with real-world situations or story problems to show the application of a particular concept in, or aspect of, the content. What would you say would be a good story or model for 1 3/4 ÷ 1/2?

The-Relationship-between-Perimeter-and-Area Scenario

Imagine that one of your students comes to class very excited. She tells you that she has figured out a theory that you never told the class. She explains that she has discovered that as a perimeter of a closed figure increases, the area also increases. She shows you this picture to prove what she is doing. How would you respond to this student?

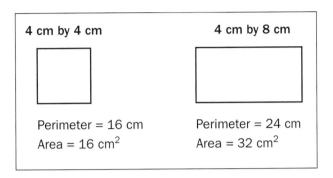

Professional-Development-Plan Task

Work with other teachers in your grade or across grades to develop a professional development plan that will support teaching a focused curriculum. Identify short- and long-term goals.

Sample-Student-Work Task

Measuring-Depth-of-Understanding Task

What might an assessment that tries to measure the depth and complexity of the division focal point for grade 5 or another focal point for grade 3, 4, or 5 look like? Develop a sample assessment task related to this focal point that you might give to students.

Appendix H

Sample Answers to Tasks

Building-Focus Task

Answers will vary. See the appendix for a listing and descriptions of the focal points identified by NCTM for grades 3, 4, and 5.

Development-of-Fractions Task

Acquiring concepts and skills for multiplication and division is a major learning progression through grades 3–5. Students also progress in their understanding of two- and three-dimensional geometric shapes and in developing measurement constructs as they relate to these shapes. Algebra readiness is also developed in grades 3–5, particularly alongside work with number and operations.

NCTM's Navigations series contains useful resources to help teachers develop students' understanding in each of the focal point areas. This appendix links the grade 3, 4, and 5 focal points to specific activities in the Navigations books. In addition, individual grade-level books on the focal points for grades 3, 4, and 5 are forthcoming from NCTM. These books will provide specific detail on the learning progressions for each of the focal points in that particular grade. A sample response for how the topic of fractions develops is presented below.

In grade 3, students develop an understanding of the meaning and uses of fractions to represent parts of a whole, parts of a set, or points or distances on a number line. Students also begin to connect fractions to division, as in fair-sharing contexts like one candy bar shared among three people. Developing the idea that the size of a fractional part is relative to the size of the whole is important. For example, one-half of a small pizza is not the same as one-half of a larger pizza. Students also develop an understanding of fraction equivalence. For example, a student might notice that if you divide a candy bar into four pieces and take two of those pieces, then that is the same as dividing that same candy bar into two pieces and taking one of the pieces. Students also begin to compare and order fractions by using models, benchmarks such as 0, 1/2, or 1, or common numerators or denominators. For example, a student may determine by looking at several models that when two fractions both have a numerator of 1, the fraction with the smaller denominator names the larger fraction. So, 1/3 of a pie is a greater amount of pie than ¼ of a pie. At the same time, a student should see that when fractions have the same denominator, the numerator names the number of equal-sized parts, and so the fraction with the larger numerator is the bigger fraction. For instance, 7/12 of a dozen doughnuts is more than 5/12 of a dozen doughnuts.

In grade 4, students connect their understanding of fractions to decimals. They investigate the relationship between fractions and decimals, focusing on equivalence. For example, students develop the understanding that 1/2 is equivalent to 5/10 and that it has a decimal representation of 0.5. They also use their knowledge of fractions as it relates to division to find decimals that are equivalent to fractions (i.e., 1/2 = 1 ÷ 2 = 0.5). Students can use a calculator to carry out the division of familiar fractions like 1/4, 1/3, 2/5, 1/2, and 3/4 to determine common fraction-decimal equivalents. Students also recognize decimal notation as an extension of the base-ten system of writing whole numbers to represent numbers between 0 and 1, between 1 and 2, and so on. They use their knowledge of the place value of whole numbers and decimals to compare and order numbers with decimals.

In grade 5, students develop fluency with the addition and subtraction of fractions and decimals. Students use their knowledge of equivalence and initial understandings of proportionality to convert to like denominators as well as other strategies. For example, to add 9/10 to 1/4, one could use the common denominator of 20 and convert to the equivalent fractions of 18/20 + 5/20 to get 23/20. An alternative and maybe easier strategy is to think of money and use $0.90 + $0.25 to get $1.15. When adding 3/4 and 3/6, one might think of a clock: 45 minutes plus 30 minutes is 75 minutes (75 minutes is 1 hour and 15 minutes or 1 1/4 hours). An alternative strategy to add 3/4 and 3/6 is to use the commutative and associative properties and also make use of commonly used fractions: 3/4 + 1/2 = (1/4 + 1/2) + 1/2 = 1 1/4.

Evaluating-My-CurriculumTask

Answers will vary.

Questioning Task

Student Assignment 1

Essential Ideas: Area measure, perimeter measure, multiplication

Teacher Questions

- Can you make a rectangle of length 5, 7, or 9? Why not?
- What multiplication fact does each rectangle represent?
- What do you notice about the area of each rectangle?
- Can you describe the rectangles with the greatest and smallest perimeters? What do they look like?

Student Assignment 2

Essential Ideas: Comparing fractions

Teacher Questions

- Can you think of a general rule to decide which fraction is bigger if they both have the same denominator?
- Can you think of a general rule to decide which fraction is bigger if they both have a numerator of 1?
- Can you think of a general rule to decide which fraction is bigger if they both have the same numerator (other than 1)?
- What strategies did you use to compare the fractions?

Student Assignment 3

Essential Ideas: Equality, equations

Teacher Questions

- Can you figure out the values of the circle or triangle from the first equation? Why or why not?
- How can the first equation be used to help you find the value of the rectangle in the second equation?
- After you find the value of the rectangle, how did you figure out the value of the circle and triangle?
- Can you write another set of equations like this for another student to solve?

Correcting-Student-Error Task

Sample response: It is clear from the student's work that he or she dropped the decimals and lined the numbers up as if adding whole numbers. You might first ask the student to explain to you how he or she added the numbers. Next, ask the student to explain what the decimal means in the number 1.14. Are 1.14 and 114 the same? You might give an example such as this: If I bought 1.14 pounds of grapes and 114 pounds of grapes, is that the same? Then, look at .089 and .3 and discuss the size of each of those numbers—is it greater than 1, less than 1, close to 0, and so on. You might look at models to represent each of the numbers. Finally, you might ask the student to come up with an estimate for the total sum and have the student compare it to his or her original answer.

Developing-Depth-of-Understanding Task

Answers will vary. Appendix F identifies specific activities from the NCTM Navigations series books that relate to the grades 3, 4, and 5 focal points.

Sample-Student-Work Task

Comparison of 5/12 and 7/12

Sample Work 1
Correct response. The student provides procedural explanation for how to compare fractions with like denominators.

Sample Work 2
The student identified the greater fraction but the explanation is unclear. The student drew a dozen doughnuts to represent each fraction but did not distinguish the fractional amounts to prove that 7/12 is larger than 5/12.

Sample Work 3
Correct response. The student represented each fraction with a set model and an area model to prove the answer. The student also justified that 7/12 is larger because if you have 7/12 of a dozen doughnuts, you would have only 5 of the dozen doughnuts remaining, whereas if you have 5/12 of a dozen doughnuts, you would have 7 doughnuts left.

Sample Work 4
Correct response. The student accurately drew a set model to represent each of the fractional amounts.

Sample Work 5
The student identified the greater fraction but converted each fraction to one with a denominator of 24 when the fractions were already like fractions with the same denominator.

Comparison of 5/6 and 5/12

Sample Work 1
The student circled the lesser fraction but the explanation seems to show that he or she knows that 5/6 is greater than 5/12. The student provides a procedural explanation on how to convert the fractions to common denominators.

Sample Work 2
Correct response. The student accurately drew an area model to represent each fraction and showed that 5/12 is the lesser fraction. The student identified 12 as a common denominator but seems to be confused about the meaning of least common denominator and greatest common denominator.

Sample Work 3
Correct response. The student represented each fraction with a length model side by side to show the larger fraction.

Sample Work 4
Correct response. The student represented each fraction with an area model to show the larger fraction and also provided a procedural explanation on how to find the least common denominator to convert to like fractions.

Comparison of 1/6 and 2/3

Sample Work 1
Correct response. The student showed procedural explanation to convert to like fractions and correctly modeled these fractions with an area model.

Sample Work 2
Correct response, although the regions, particularly in the second fraction, are not equal. More than half of the second pie should be shaded in to represent 2/3.

Sample Work 3
Correct response. The student accurately drew an area model to represent each fraction and also showed that 2/3 is closer to a whole than 1/6.

Sample Work 4
Correct answer, and the student showed how to convert one of the fractions to a common denominator; however, the drawing of 2/3 of a pizza is not accurate. The student's comment "3 quarters of the pizza is better than 1" is also unclear.

Find the Unknown Value

Sample Work 1

Incorrect response. The student looked at each expression separately and plugged in numbers that would make the expression true.

Sample Work 2

Partially correct response. The student correctly determined the value of the rectangle in the second equation by substituting the known sum of the circle and triangle; however, the student made a computational error in calculating the value of the circle, which also gave him or her an incorrect value for the triangle.

Sample Work 3

Correct response. The student correctly used the sum from the first equation to determine the value of the rectangle in the second equation and then used that information to determine the other two unknown values.

Sample Work 4

Correct answers, but the student seemed to use a guess-and-check approach until she found numbers that worked rather than substitute the first sum into the second equation to determine the value of the rectangle.

Knowing and Teaching Elementary School Mathematics Tasks
Multidigit-Multiplication Scenario

Sample response

First, you might ask the student to tell you the value of each digit in 645: the 5 is in the ones place and stands for five ones; the 4 is in the tens place and stands for four tens, or 40; and the 6 is in the hundreds place and stands for six hundreds, or 600. Next, break the problem down into the three subproblems of 123 × 5, 123 × 40, and 123 × 600 and solve each of these problems and compare to what the student originally had for each partial product. You might model how to perform the calculation using the standard algorithm and discuss the reason for "moving the numbers over" after each step or adding zeros (i.e., the 492 represents 492 tens, or 4,920). You might also give the student additional practice with multiplying by powers of 10 and discuss the patterns (i.e., when multiplying a number by 10, we put one zero after the number; multiplying by 100, we put two zeros after the number; and so on).

The Relationship-between-Perimeter-and-Area Scenario

First, you might engage the student in investigating her claim with other examples to see whether it still holds true. For example, ask the student to draw rectangles that have an area of 20. Then ask the student to find the perimeters of those figures. The student might come up with the following drawings. From these examples, the student will see that as the perimeter increases, the area stays the same.

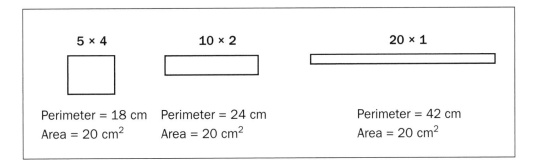

Next, you might ask the student to see if she can come up with any rectangles that have a perimeter greater than 16 cm but an area less than 16 cm² to compare to her original 4 × 4 square. You might come up with the following rectangles for the comparison, which shows that the perimeter can increase as the area decreases.

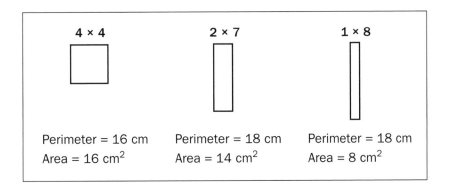

Finally, you might ask the student to compare the rectangles for which an increase in the perimeter resulted in an increase in the area to those for which an increase in perimeter resulted in a decrease in, or no change to, the area. How did the lengths and widths change? From this comparison, you might lead the student to conjecture that when the increase in perimeter is caused by an increase in the length or width of the rectangle, or both, the area of the figure will change accordingly. However, if the increase in perimeter is caused by increasing the length and decreasing the width, or vice versa, the area could increase, decrease, or stay the same.

Professional-Development-Plan Task

Short-Term Goals

- Attend monthly meetings with my grade-level team to plan lessons and activities related to the identified focal point areas.

- Attend schoolwide and cross-grade-level meetings to discuss focal points and the growth of knowledge across the grades.

- Attend one or two professional development offerings or courses related to an identified focal point area for my grade level.

Long-Term Goals

- Continue to increase mathematics content knowledge by taking professional development offerings or courses related to the focal point areas for my grade level.

- Work with the principal and other school administrators to support new teachers in teaching a focused curriculum.

- Build a library of resources for supporting the teaching of a focused mathematics curriculum.

Measuring-Depth-of-Understanding Task

Sample Assessment Task for Understanding the Concept of Division (Grade-3 Focal Point)

Understanding the Concept of Division	
Do the students understand what division means? Can the students interpret different representations of division? For example: • Partitioning, or sharing—If there are 6 cookies and 2 people, how many will each person get? • Measuring, or repeated subtraction—If you have 6 cookies and want each person to get 3 cookies, how many people will get cookies?	Take 35 blocks. Use the blocks to show how to do this problem: $35 \div 7 =$ Solve these two problems and explain how they are alike or different: • If you divide 35 blocks into 7 groups, how many will be in each group? • If you put 35 blocks into groups of 7, how many groups will there be? Solve these two problems and explain how they are alike or different: • José had 6 children at his party. How would he divide 25 cookies among them? • Jamie wanted each child in the game to have 6 marbles. She had 25 marbles. How many children could be in the game? Source: *Mathematics Assessment: A Practical Handbook for Grades 3–5* (NCTM 2001, p. 9)
Assessment questions: • Did students distinguish between the two forms of division? • Were their block arrangements or explanations accurate and explanatory? • Do they understand how division by grouping and by distributing are alike and different?	

References

Hiebert, James, Thomas P. Carpenter, Elizabeth Fennema, Karen C. Fuson, Diana Wearne, Hanlie Murray, Alwyn Olivier, and Piet Human. *Making Sense: Teaching and Learning Mathematics with Understanding.* Portsmouth, N.H.: Heinemann, 1997.

Ma, Liping. *Knowing and Teaching Elementary Mathematics: Teachers' Understanding of Fundamental Mathematics in China and the United States.* Mahwah, N.J.: Lawrence Erlbaum Associates, 1999.

National Council of Teachers of Mathematics (NCTM). *Mathematics Teaching Today: Improving Practice, Improving Student Learning,* 2nd edition, edited by Tami S. Martin. Reston, Va.: NCTM, 2007a.

———. *Navigating through Number and Operations in Grades 3–5,* edited by Francis (Skip) Fennell. Reston, Va.: NCTM, 2007b.

———. *Curriculum Focal Points for Prekindergarten through Grade 8: A Quest for Coherence.* Reston, Va.: NCTM, 2006.

———. *Mathematics Assessment Sampler, Grades 3–5,* edited by Jane D. Gawronski. Reston, Va.: NCTM, 2005.

———. *Principles and Standards for School Mathematics.* Reston, Va.: NCTM, 2000.

———. *Curriculum and Evaluation Standards for School Mathematics.* Reston, Va.: NCTM, 1989.

National Mathematics Advisory Panel. "Learning Progresses Progress Report, September 2007." Available from http://www.ed.gov/about/bdscomm/list/mathpanel/8th-meeting/presentations/progressreports.html. Internet; accessed 12 December 2007.

Shulman, Lee S. "Those Who Understand: Knowledge Growth in Teaching." *Educational Researcher* 15 (February 1986): 4–14.